The Culture of Sexism

Recent Titles in
Human Evolution, Behavior, and Intelligence

The Culture of Sexism

Ignacio L. Götz

Human Evolution, Behavior, and Intelligence
Seymour W. Itzkoff, Series Editor

PRAEGER

Westport, Connecticut
London

Library of Congress Cataloging-in-Publication Data

Götz, Ignacio L.
   The culture of sexism / Ignacio L. Götz.
      p.   cm.—(Human evolution, behavior, and intelligence, ISSN
1063–2158)
   Includes bibliographical references.
   ISBN 0–275–96566–X (alk. paper)
   1. Sexism.   2. Sexism in religion.   3. Sexism in literature.
   I. Title. II. Series.
   HQ23.G7   1999
   305.3—dc21   99–21598

British Library Cataloguing in Publication Data is available.

Library of Congress Catalog Card Number: 99–21598
ISBN: 0–275–96566–X
ISSN: 1063–2158

First published in 1999

Praeger Publishers, 88 Post Road West, Westport, CT 06881
An imprint of Greenwood Publishing Group, Inc.
www.praeger.com

Printed in the United States of America

The paper used in this book complies with the
Permanent Paper Standard issued by the National
Information Standards Organization (Z39.48–1984).

10 9 8 7 6 5 4 3 2 1

For

Ilse, Kathy, Chris, Marce, Soy

Ob Mutter? Tochter? Schwester? Enkelin?
Die Gott-Natur enthüllt sich zum Gewinn
(Goethe, "Kore")

There appear to be themes of such strangeness
that rational men will ignore them,
preferring to take off on some tangent.

Erik Erikson, Identity: Youth and Crisis

Contents

Acknowledgments

I am grateful to those who helped me gain an understanding of the complexities of sexism, especially my colleagues, my students, and my family. Ralph Page, from the University of Illinois, encouraged me to write, and Seymour Itzkoff was gracious enough to sponsor my ideas. My editor, James T. Sabin, has offered the guidance I needed to bring this project to fruition, and Lynne Ann Goetz has gently steered it to completion.

Besides these, grateful acknowledgment is made to the following for permission to reprint (sometimes upon payment of a fee) previously published material:

The Johns Hopkins University Press for permission to quote from *The Mothers in FAUST*, by Harold Jantz. Copyright © 1969.

Diane Wolkstein for permission to quote from *Inanna: Queen of Heaven and Earth*, by Diane Wolkstein and Samuel N. Kramer, published by HarperCollins Publishers, Inc. Copyright © 1983.

Penguin Books, Ltd., for permission to quote from *The Epic of Gilgamesh*, translated by N. K. Sandars (Penguin Classics 1960, Third Edition 1972). Copyright © N.K. Sandars, 1960, 1964, 1972.

Introduction

This book represents an effort to deal with sexism, which I take to mean here unjustified preference of one sex and its functions over the other (Lerner 240-242). The main purpose is to understand why contemporary societies continue to be sexist despite efforts to correct the bias. A major part of the problem is that sexism is rooted in a society's culture and not only in its institutions. Moreover, sexism has been a part of culture for several thousand years, so that its forms have become refined, its most insidious expressions subtle; therefore a steady, protracted, and penetrating analysis is required to uncover it.

I want to look at some of these underlying conditions of sexism in our culture, using as evidence materials from several pertinent disciplines, primarily from within the humanities. I hope these will throw some light on sexism.

I am aware that the views presented here are not the usual ones. Current discussion of sexism centers around psychosocial interpretations, ranging from extreme visions of society and its mechanisms to the very conservative religious views that maintain that nothing is the matter.

The major trends seem to be two, religious and secular. The latter orientation examines sexism from the point of view of politics, economics, social pressures and organizations, psychological make-ups, and the like. Within each of these disciplines there are many subdivisions that hearken back to preferred theories or theorists. Thus there are the more Marxist or leftist critiques generally dubbed radical and subsumed under "radical feminism." Writers within this group view sexism as inextricably twined with the capitalistic structures of modern societies, and its elimination as dependent upon some revolutionary activity and some more humane and egalitarian reconstruction of society. Some view sexism as more directly connected with the exercise of power, economic and political. Sexism, then, would be the outcome of an uneven sharing of power based on an uneven distribution of the economic means, and it could be eliminated only through an empowering of women at the economic and political levels. Some view sexism as endemic in long-established social practices and arrangements that dictate rigid and stereotypical roles from which it is not possible to diverge. These roles are often seen as the cause of psychological orientations, preconceptions, perspectives, and self-concepts, which trap men and women in their specific roles *from the inside*, as it were.

The religious point of view, on the other hand, seeks to understand sexism from the perspective of what is termed patriarchal religion. The advent of Indo-European hordes on the scene of an agriculturalist world some seven thousand years ago, a world whose worship centered around the Goddess and whose peaceful culture abounded in the production of art, introduced conceptions of the deity that were predominantly male, and generated a culture overwhelmingly warlike. Civilization, the turning of humans into city dwellers, had ushered in the privatization of women, and this movement was enhanced and rigidified by the new patriarchy. With the worship of a male god came the banning of the goddess, and with the spread of Judaism, Christianity, and Islam throughout the world, came the predominance of an ideology that saw male power as divine and female weakness as temptation. Sexism is but the outcome of this patriarchal ideology; as long as the ideology exists, and as long as its domination of the human mind continues, sexism will persist.

There are, of course, those who insist that this ideology is sacrosanct, that it is revealed truth, spoken to leaders and visionaries from Moses to the Prophet Smith. Sexism, for them, does not really exist. God has determined that women shall be subordinate, and has declared so in the Bible, or the Koran, or the Book of Mormon. Such people are unwilling to entertain the notion that these books, too, bear the influence of the social prejudices of the times when they were written, and that they were written during patriarchal times.

I do not question the legitimacy of the more secular assessments of sexism. I believe that a phenomenon as complex and pervasive as sexism must needs be examined from as many points of view as possible. If sexism has developed over a period of some twelve thousand years — as is likely — it must have affected the whole fabric of social life and not just a few facets. Therefore all the various disciplines whose task is the study of social living have something to contribute to our understanding of it and our efforts to eliminate it.

My concern is that in a predominantly secular and exterior culture, there is a tendency to neglect the effects of interior factors, especially those of a more religious nature. But there can be no doubt that religious ideologies have played a very important role in the justification and maintenance of sexism. There can be no doubt, either, that religious ideologies continue to be important factors in the ongoing existence and legitimation of sexism.

It is to these more religious factors that I have tried to address myself, not because I think the secular ones are irrelevant, but because I think the ideological ones are equally important. Among these religious/ideological factors, I have chosen to deal with the more esoteric ones that appear in mythology, legend, and fairy tale. I have also tried to deal with somewhat more abstract or more recondite categories such as creativity and receptivity, for it seems to me that an analysis of these, too, can enhance our understanding of sexism and, perhaps, hasten its elimination. But this choice of topic renders my study somewhat unorthodox, for it is often thought, especially by the trendier analysts and spokespersons of the day (let alone the general public) that mythology and fairy tales are things of the past, unworthy of study in an age of enlightened scientific research. And yet it may be true, as Camille Paglia claims (Chapter 1), that political and socioeconomic equality will *not* remedy the problems of sexism because the point of it all is *not* equality, but justice.

I first presented the kernel of the ideas contained here in another book, *Creativity: Theoretical and Socio-Cosmic Reflections* (1978). The encouragement of colleagues and friends led to the expansion of those ideas into the present book. I also felt the need to develop more fully the arguments sketched there. This applied most specifically to the segments on mythology — that is, to the subconscious levels at which the fear and envy of women's receptivity is operative in perpetuating sexism.

The work done in this presentation of mythological, legendary, and fairy tale materials is not exhaustive — not by a long shot. A great deal of work is being done in this area, and much more will have to be done before the entire picture is clear. But I believe I have done sufficient work to demonstrate the existence of this subconscious envy of female receptivity, so that other more patient researchers may enlarge and complete the task. This will help all of us obtain an even more comprehensive view of sexism and its underlying (though subconscious) rationale.

The core of the book is the view that sexism arises, at least in part, out of a subconscious male envy of female receptivity; briefly, out of womb envy, conceived as representing the distinctive female capacity to receive. The obvious ground of this envy is the realization in the growing boy that women have something he lacks (Chapter 1).

This subconscious envy is documented by reference to a variety of mythological motifs, fairy tales, and religious beliefs, especially, but not exclusively, within the Western tradition. The importance of mythology, especially, is the fact that it bears naive witness to people's real beliefs. Thus it becomes a good proof of the hypothesis of womb envy (Chapters 2 to 5).

In the latter part of the book I explore briefly the psychological mechanisms operative in the formation of womb envy (Chapter 6), and take a look at schooling as one institution that perhaps unwittingly perpetuates the womb envy that is so much a part of sexism (Chapter 7). Some issues relating to technology and gender are discussed in Chapter 8, and a concluding chapter rounds up the argument.

Chapter 1

Make War, Not Love

In Roger O. Hirson's musical *Pippin*, a very funny exchange takes place between Pippin and his grandmother, Berthe. Berthe, who has not seen Pippin for some time, asks him where he has been.

> *Pippin*: I went to war, Grandma.
> *Berthe*: No wonder you look so terrible. Men and their
> wars. Sometimes I think men raise flags when they
> can't get anything else up.
> *Pippin*: Grandma, sometimes you really say shocking things.
> *Berthe*: I try my best.

Berthe's comment about the connection between war and sex is more profound than it appears at first hearing. It is the task of the present chapter to explore some of its implications. Do men, indeed, raise flags because they cannot raise anything else? Or do they raise flags and make wars to counter the effects of women's childbearing?

WAR AND MOTHERHOOD

In a seminal essay, Nancy Huston (1986) has explored the subtle connection between war and childbirth. Huston's argument is based on the obtrusive nature of motherhood in primitive societies, and the apprehension by males that they cannot give birth. This apprehension of limitation leads men to devise activities that will somehow approximate the experience of giving birth. It also leads men to search for themselves a characteristic as distinctive as childbirth is for women (Lerner 45-46). According to Huston, war-making ends up being as distinctive for men as motherhood is for women. The data upon which Huston bases her constructs are plentiful, and I can only summarize a few of them here, adding some of my own that I feel are relevant.

The preferment of war over motherhood seems to have begun in very ancient times, but it is very clearly discernible as successive waves of Indo-European or "Kurgan" invasions took place between *ca.* 4400 and 2900 B.C.E. The

Goddess-centered, matrifocal civilization of Old Europe and the Middle East, with its emphasis on agriculture, on art, and on domestication (Lerner 46), was slowly destroyed and/or superseded by the patrilinear pastoralists from the steppes (a transition probably captured centuries later by the Biblical story of Cain and Abel and by the Sumerian myth of Dumuzi and Enkimdu). The invaders were seminomadic and more primitive than the people they overran, and their religious orientation was both male and combative. Marija Gimbutas writes,

> The new ideology was an apotheosis of the horseman and warrior. The principal gods carried weapons and rode horses and chariots; they were figures of inexhaustible energy, physical power, and fecundity. . . . They carried shining daggers, swords, and shields . . . [and] glorified the magical swiftness of arrow and javelin and the sharpness of the blade (Gimbutas, "Women and Culture," 31).

The "new" orientation toward war appeared also in certain parts or aspects of even more ancient initiation rites for boys. These had as their main objective not merely the introduction of the boy to adult society, but equally the preparation of the boy to assume the responsibilities of adult *males* in the conduct of war. This is clear from the particulars of the rites themselves, such as fasting, hunting, ritual dances (both of war and of hunting), investitures, and the like. For girls, on the other hand, initiation is designed to prepare them for their perceived main role as adult women, namely, motherhood. One could say that initiation rites prepare boys for production in work and war, and girls for reproduction in motherhood. War and motherhood, production and repro-duction, seem to be the fundamental modes of a society's existence, as Frederick Engels maintained. As he put it, "according to the materialistic conception, the determining factor in history is, in the final instance, the production and reproduction of immediate life" (Engels, "The Part," 455; Lerner 21 *ff.* and 40-41; Chodorow; Dinnerstein; Gottlieb).[1] Our history, in other words, is determined by the way we work and the way we reproduce — really, by the modes of work and sex.

Engels did not imply that these modes were divided, production being in the hands of men, reproduction in the hands of women. His point was, rather, that although work and sex were universals, the ways in which work was organized, and the patterns of sexual relationships, determined the social mode of the life of the groups, and rendered them different.

Huston's point, with which I agree, goes further. It maintains that the modes of production and reproduction have been split and apportioned along gender lines; that the reason for this split is male envy of motherhood (or the desire to compensate through male production for the reproductive power women have); that this apportioning is evident in initiation rites; and that it is discernible in other social practices.

At the adult level, the search for a characteristic male mode is documented by a number of phenomena that involve the appropriation of women in marriage (Stannard 313-319) and of feminine corporeal signs connected with motherhood. The primary example is *couvade*, the widespread practice among primitive peoples, in which the father would go to bed at the time of the birth of his child, complaining of labor pains, observing dietary restrictions, and otherwise acting like a woman who has given birth (Stannard 290, 324).[2] But there are other examples imbedded in language, the clearest one being the equation of the pain of warfare with the pain of childbirth, a simile used repeatedly in heroic literature. From it there have developed a multitude of expressions which equate war and revolution with giving birth to new societies, and that cast the revolutionary in the role of midwife. Even in the harmless battle of wits, Socrates saw his own role as that of a midwife, helping people give birth to their ideas.

To endure the pains of war is for a man what for a woman is to endure the pains of childbirth, and men are masculine when they do so without fear in the same manner as women prove themselves feminine when they give birth in tears. "Given that women are 'marked' by their capacity for having children," writes Huston, "men have been compelled to find a similarly distinctive trait for themselves, something that could ratify, as it were, their masculinity" (Huston, "Matrix," 127). That distinctive trait is war-making, and the machismo that goes with it.

Concomitantly, there is in the extant poetic and dramatic literature a clear preference for war over motherhood, manifest in both the exaltation of war and the degradation of motherhood. For example, the Amazons, who in ancient times are said to have inhabited Lybia, Anatolia, and the shores of the Black Sea, as well as the island of Lemnos, were reputed to be warlike and to prefer their wars to more maternal activities. In northern Europe, the Valkyries were the equivalent of the Amazons. These warrior-maidens subserved the purposes of war in that they chose the heroes to be slain in battle, and carried them to Valhalla, the "Hall of the Slain," where they feast and joust forever. War becomes the eternal reward of the warrior; heaven is a battlefield. Women are praised when they support war, help in it, sacrifice their children to it, and encourage them to be heroic. Spartan women are said to have told their children as they went to war, "Return with your shield or on it!" and the remark became famous. "The men must see to the fighting," Hector tells Andromache (*Iliad*, VI.443). And what do women do? They are a pretext for war (as in the case of Helen of Troy); they serve as booty and/or recompense; they may be "property" to be defended; in their brothels, they are solace to tired warriors; they are casualties, both in death and in rape (the Achaeans swear not to return home until each has raped the wife of a Trojan [*Iliad*, II.355]); they are spies, nurses, or simply passive spectators whose tears provide contrast to the atrocities of war. And, of course, they listen to war narratives. In fact, says Huston, "it is much less significant that men's History is made of wars than that men's wars are made of stories" ("Tales," 271).

Even though the pains of childbirth are acknowledged, those of war are preferred. "I only say with Euripides," writes Sóren Kierkegaard: "I would rather go through war three times than through childbirth once" (Kierkegaard, I, 430; Euripides, *Medea*, 240). So men willingly go to war, and the king who champions it becomes the father of his people. In some instances, as in the case of the Hebrews at the time of David, war becomes a holy activity, and the soldiers abstain from sexual contact while on duty (*2 Sam.* 11:8-11): war is more important than sex. (Until recently, football players preparing for the Superbowl were sequestered from their wives for a week!)

The preference and glorification of war over sex is an old one. Eve is cursed with motherhood and Adam with labor (*Gen.* 3:16-19), but YHWH is a man of war (*Exod.* 15:3), mighty in battle (*Ps.* 24:8), and Israel's enemies are his enemies. For the Muslims, to join in war for Allah is a holy act, and whether they win or lose, they earn eternal rewards (*Qu'rân*, Sûrah IV.74). For Aquinas war can be justified if it is commanded by the proper authority, for a just cause, and undertaken with the right intention (*STh* 2-2, 40, 1c). The idea of a Holy War arises, thus, in Judaism, in Islam, and in Christianity (Stackhouse)[3] — and not just in theory. On the eve of the Battle of the Mulvian Bridge (312), Constantine had a vision of a flaming cross and of the words, in Greek, "You will conquer by this Sign." The next day his legions marched into battle with painted crosses on their banners, while Maxentius's soldiers went to defeat under the standard of Mithra. A thousand years later, most of the world had been conquered in the name of Allah, though holy wars of reconquest — the Crusades — had mobilized Christian Europe against the Moor. In fact, as the saga of El Cid makes abundantly clear, the universal feeling among Christians of the time was that "by garroting Moors, God was glorified."

The same conviction permeated the soldiers and sailors of the Spanish Armada in the English Channel as well as at Lepanto. Similarly, at the start of Britain's entry into World War II, Bishop Dey, in a Pastoral Letter to the Chaplains and men of His Majesty's Forces, September 23, 1939, could call the men "fortunate in this, that the cause which summons you to arms is right and just in the eyes of God and of all good men; therefore, you may engage in battle with a quiet conscience and firm trust that God will bless you in the performance of your duty."

Even though for men war becomes the equivalent of motherhood, to make sure war is seen as most important there is an obvious attempt to downplay the importance of motherhood. For Aquinas, as for Aristotle (*De Generat. Animal.*, II.3 [737^a 27]), woman is "a misbegotten male" (*STh* 1, 99, 2 *ad* 1) whose contribution to motherhood is purely passive (*STh* 1, 98, 2c). Motherhood itself is not necessary for marriage (*STh* 3, 29, 2); in fact, virginal or sexless marriage, like that of Mary and Joseph, is the ideal (Gold 102-117). Further, human life is said to originate not only from women but also from nonhuman objects like stones, or even from men themselves. We have, thus, a large number of myths in which humans are created from stones, from dragons' teeth, or from men, as in the myth of the birth of Dionysus (from Zeus's thigh) and of Athena (from Zeus's head), and in the Biblical story of the creation of Eve from Adam's rib.   Again, women do not even need to be conscious for pregnancy to occur, as many stories of intercourse with seemingly dead maidens who become pregnant attest. It is as if men sought to deny the very obvious and very important role played by women in reproduction; to skirt the issues raised by it; "or to attribute to themselves the specifically female and somewhat terrifying power of giving birth" (Huston, "Matrix," 126; Phillips 89).

That this is an effort and not a mere accident is apparent from the fact that in many cases the myths are rewritten or retold, or certain elements are omitted, so as to gloss over or obliterate the role of women.   Aeschylus, for example, in the *Eumenides*, has Athena born directly from the head of Zeus without a woman's help:

> APOLLO:
> The woman you call the mother of   666
> the child is not the parent, just a
> nurse to the seed, the new-born seed
> that grows and swells inside her.
> The man is the source of life . . .
> I give you proof that all I say is   672
> true: the father can father without a
> mother. Here she stands, our living
> witness. Look —
>
>   [Exhibiting Athena]
>
> Child sprung full-blown from Olympian
> Zeus, never bred in the darkness of the
> womb.   676

Later on in the play Athena herself proclaims the myth:

> ATHENA:
> No mother gave me birth.   751

But the fact is that this is a late or rewritten version of the myth.   The original involves Metis, Zeus's first wife, who being with child, warns her husband that her child may some day overpower him (as Zeus overpowered his own father); so Zeus swallows her up, and when the time is up, Zeus brings the child forth as his own. The child is, indeed, Athena, but she is by no means a creature "never bred in the darkness of the womb."   Examples of this kind abound, from the substitution of male-administered baptism (spiritual birth) for birth, and the belief that semen carries "homunculi" (little humans) to be deposited in the womb (so that women's role is that of a mere repository), all the way to the still prevalent custom of giving newborn children their father's surname (Stannard 289, 294).

SOME QUESTIONS

For the past few thousand years the preferences of men have become the cultural values of humanity as a whole (Huston, "Matrix," 133; Morgan 70). War has been a predominant factor during the reign of patriarchy. But the fact that men cannot give birth explains only partially their preference for war. Even allowing for the elements of pain and bloodshed as important factors in the substitution of war for motherhood, the partiality remains. After all, there *are* other forms of male creativeness, such as the arts, manufacture, politics, and sports, which involve sweat, tears, and even bloodshed. Moreover, many ancient goddesses were warring deities: Sekhmet in Egypt; Inanna in Sumer; Anath in Uruk; the Morrigan in Ireland; Kali in India; Bellona in Rome; Athena in Greece. So why would war have been chosen over other forms of productivity? This question Huston does not answer; she does not even raise it.

I am not saying she is wrong. In fact, I believe she is right, and that her essay explains a lot of what otherwise remains unexplainable in the history of culture and in the present world. But is there something else? Could it be that the male preference for war may be explained more profoundly by the male inability to receive than by his inability to give birth? Could it be that what is threatening to men is not so much the creativity of birthing as the open, engorged womb — the fact that without war and childbirth the gaping gap of possibility is suddenly thrust into prominence? Could it be that more fundamental than the desire to substitute war (male creativity) for motherhood (female creativity) is the desire to obliterate receptivity (the female womb)? Could it be that the hidden main-spring of patriarchy *in general* (and not merely of war) is womb envy, not in so far as the womb is mothering, but in so far as it is receptive? Could it be that the male emphasis on creativity, especially war, is (to borrow Nietzsche's words) "the revolt of the underprivileged" (Nietzsche, *Will*, #179), "the tyrannomania of impotence" (Nietzsche, *Zarathustra*, II.7, 100)?

NOTES

1. This matter has been hotly debated. See "An exchange: Mothering and the Reproduction of Power," *Socialist Review* 14:6 (November-December 1984): 121-130.

2. As Claude Lévi-Strauss, *The Savage Mind* (Chicago: Chicago University Press, 1968), p. 195, points out, it is not so much that the husband takes the place of the wife as that he acts in a manner similar to hers. This difference does not affect the present argument.

3. Evidence suggests that the sanctification of war was a result of the Indo-European invasions. The invaders from the North, whose distinctive symbols were the thunderbolt and the pine tree, considered death in battle a boon from heaven. For other reasons and examples, especially pertaining to the extraordinary militarism of Christianity, see John Boswell, *Same-Sex Unions in Premodern Europe* (New York: Villard Books, 1994), 156-161.

Chapter 2

Male Creativity and Female Receptivity: Some Data

We must now proceed to clarify and define some of the terms used so far, and to substantiate certain connections. What is masculinity? What is femininity? How are creativity and receptivity defined? On what grounds can one connect masculinity with creativity, and receptivity with femininity?

CREATIVITY AND RECEPTIVITY

Creativity is the process or activity of deliberately concretizing insight (Götz, "Defining Creativity," 300). Receptivity is potentiality, capacity, ability; it is the no-thing-ness of things before they are. Put differently, creativity is the process by which the imagination stands out (*ex-sists*) in the world, or by which fantasy is turned into reality. To imagine is to envisage openings; to create is to erect, to intrude physically into the world, to fill.

The imagination is essentially the human consciousness's capacity to differentiate, to negate, or as Sartre has it, to nihilate (Sartre, *Imagination*, 135). It is the human consciousness's capacity to say "I am *not* you," or to "see" in a block of marble what is not yet, what does not yet exist, namely, the lineaments of a statue. The imagination is the capacity to envisage voids of possibility, emptinesses that can be filled. It is also the power to see form-lessness behind form, potency before act; to return, as in Taoism, to the "Uncarved Block." Creativity, on the other hand, is the process by which such imaginings are concretized, regardless of the field. Wrote Shakespeare:

> . . . as imagination bodies forth
> the forms of things unknown, the poet's pen
> turns them to shape and gives to airy nothing
> a local habitation and a name.
> (*A Midsummer-Night's Dream* V.1, 14-17)

The process by which the poet's pen (or the sculptor's chisel; or the painter's brush; or the person's actions, generally) concretizes the airy nothings, is the process of creativity.

But there is more, for I maintain that the intrusive character of creativity corresponds to the masculine, while the open nature of receptivity corresponds to the feminine. However, before such correspondence can be established, there is need to define the masculine and the feminine.

MASCULINITY AND FEMININITY

In a most fundamental way, we are consciously acting sexual beings (Ortega y Gasset, *Man and People*, 128-129). That is to say: even though one must first be, exist, maintain oneself alive before one can *act* sexually in a deliberate way, one first *is* sexual, male or female. It is in this prior mode of sexual being, I think, that the most fundamental characterization of the masculine and the feminine is to be found. Put differently, the only culture-free characterization of the masculine and the feminine is anatomical. Masculine is anatomical male; feminine is anatomical female. By anatomical I mean the actual bodily configuration of males and females. This must be the case because in prehistorical times there was no knowledge of hormones, chromosomes, or other determining scientific factors, yet there obviously was a differentiation between men and women.[1]

This conclusion is inescapable; but is it significant? Or is it merely tautological? The answer will depend on whether or not it is possible to specify characteristics which flow intimately from male and female anatomy. The question, therefore, is this: Is it possible to ground on male anatomy a group of characteristics that could be referred to as masculine, and is it possible to ground on female anatomy another group of characteristics that could be called feminine?

Male sexual anatomy is characterized by its intrusiveness; female sexual anatomy by its receptiveness. "Taking the insertive role in sexual intercourse . . . is male-typical behavior. Taking the receptive role is, for men, sexatypical behavior" (LeVay 71). Receptiveness is female-typical. As Erik Erikson says of women, "Their somatic design harbors an 'inner space'" (Erikson, *Identity*, 266; Ortega y Gasset, *Man and People*, 130-131).

Our awareness of ourselves in the world is built fundamentally on the experience of our physical interaction with the world. As somatic configurations differ between male and female, an infant boy's and an infant girl's (and later a man's and a woman's) interactions with the world will differ. In Christine Allen's words, "it 'feels' different to be a woman or a man. The female body and the male body give rise to different experiences of the world."

The different experiences or interactions ground a different sense of self as masculine or feminine. Such a sense of what is masculine (i.e., intrusive or creative) and of what is feminine (i.e., receptive) is, initially at least, grounded on nature (i.e., anatomy) and not on the artificial impositions of society and culture. It is safe to assume, I think, that if artificial impositions from culture were not superimposed on the natural interrelationship with the environment of males and females to the point of obscuring it, the sense of what is masculine and feminine would be grounded more directly (though obviously not exclusively) on somatic configurations as these condition our interaction with the world.

I am emphasizing here the physiological grounds of femaleness and maleness, and for obvious reasons, I think. But this does not deny the influence of nurture and environment on the sexual sense of self, about which I will say more later. Still, as Erich Neumann puts it,

> The totality of the psyche, the center of which is the Self, exists in a relationship of identity with the body, the vehicle of the psychic process. . . . Hence between the sexes we must assume a biopsychic difference that is manifested in archetypal and symbolic ways. . . . Therefore the Self as the totality of the personality rightly carries secondary sexual characteristics, and both body and psyche are closely connected in their dependence on hormones (*Fear* 6-7).

My position may be termed modified or moderate essentialism (Sheets-Johnstone 39-47; Paglia Chapter 1; LeVay Chapter 9; Epstein; Nadeau). While I hold that there is a physiological ground for gender identity, I also admit that becoming a man or a woman does not take place in a neutral environment. To deny the latter is unrealistic; to give up the former is to resign oneself to a hopeless relativism that renders social criticism ultimately ineffectual.

LINK: THE EVIDENCE

What evidence do we have to link creativity with maleness and receptivity with femaleness? Historically, the earliest experiences of creativity must have been associated with childbirth. Here was this being whose inner recesses engorged themselves until suddenly, after a very long time, a new creature was extruded into the world. Birthing was creating new humans. The fascination with this gorging of the womb and its emptying into the world is captured, I think, in the dozens of statuettes of pregnant women found along northern Europe and into Russia, dating back to *ca.* 35,000 B.C.E.

Then came the cave paintings — Lascaux, Altamira, Nerja, and later Tassili; paintings of single animals and of herds on the walls of womb-like caves — perhaps as a prayerful wish that these imaginary herds, gestating in the innards of Mother Earth, might soon materialize in the upper world (as the child materialized out of the womb) to become the object of a hunt (Campbell, *Historical*, II.1, 10).

These are the beginnings, the few inklings we have into our remote past. But it is obvious from the mythologies that developed subsequently that the experience of creativity was far more complicated than that. The complementarity of male and female, apparent in the Lascaux caves (Campbell, *Historical*, I.1, 59-62) and in the most ancient mythologies, is only one aspect, but there must have been others. Men, after all, did not swell up, only women did; men did not bring new human beings into the world, only women did; men did not have the inner receptacle needed for gestation; only women did. Even though a merging of the sexual organs may have been necessary for the creation of human life, men have lacked the distinctive capacity to receive. *Distinctive* is the operative term here. Men lacked female reproductive, or vagina-womb, systems. They could substitute their own productions for the female production of babies; they could create, indeed — tools, paintings, villages, all on the analogy of childbirth; they could also "make" war; but they could not receive distinctively. Only woman could do this.

The most ancient mythologies corroborate this perception: creation is erection, and therefore it is characteristic of the male; reception is womb-like, and therefore it is characteristic of the female. In the *Yi Ching* the fundamental trigrams are based on *yin* (the feminine, represented by the broken line — —) and *yang* (the masculine, represented by the unbroken line ————). The first hexagram, made up of six unbroken *yang* lines is *Ch'ien*, the Creative, "heaven." Visually it is massive, erectable; the second is *K'un*, the Receptive, "Earth." It consists of six broken *yin* lines and it is visually open, like a slit.

In the *Shuo Kua* 7 and 9, we read: "The Creative is strong. The Receptive is accepting. . . . The Creative is heaven, therefore it is called the father. The Receptive is the earth, therefore it is called the mother."

In Vedanta Hinduism, the receptive vulva (*yoni*) is the symbol of the female. Sometimes what is symbolized by the *yoni* is the birthing property of the womb rather than its receptivity. After all, Hinduism bears the mark of the invading, patrifocal Indo-Europeans. Swâmî Karapâtrî explains: "the symbol of the Supreme-Man (*purusha*), the formless, the changeless, the all-seeing eye, is the symbol of masculinity, the phallus or *linga*. The symbol of the power that is Nature, generatrix of all that exists, is the female organ, the *yoni*" (Karapâtrî, "Lingopâsanâ-rahasya," 154). Mythologically, Karapâtrî states elsewhere, the love of Krishna and Râdha "is an allegory of the cosmic union of the Supreme-Man (*purusha*) with Nature (*prakriti*), from which the universe gradually arose" (Karapâtrî, "Krishna tattva"). Sometimes, however, the *yoni* represents female receptivity pure and simple, as in the mandalas and the myriad aniconic symbols sculpted in temples or discovered among certain fruits (some coconuts, for example). Even in the regular, iconic statuary and pictorial representations, the receptive is often explicit, as in the statues and paintings of the Kali *yantra*, and of Kali astride the Shiva corpse, her *yoni* sucking his inert *linga*.

It is clear that the female organ lends itself to a dual symbolism. It is bipolar, creative and receptive. Nancy Huston (*Matrix*), contrasts the creativity of the female (womb) with the creativity of the male: men make war as women make babies. But a more fundamental contrast exists, I think, between the distinctive *receptivity* of the *yoni* and the *creativity* of the *linga*.

The dualism of some female symbols is apparent, for example, in the fact that the Mother Goddess, Earth, is said to receive the dead in her womb. In fact, megalithic burial places were often constructed in the shape of a round womb, with a passage leading into it through which the remains of the deceased were carried. Such is the case in Scandinavian mythology and burial practices (Davidson 20). Some Celtic temples/tombs also reflect this purely receptive symbolism. They are constructed as underground chambers with long passages leading in. The construction is so precise as to allow one bright ray of rising sun to penetrate fully to the depths on only one particular day, once a year, usually December 21. A case in point is Newgrange, in Ireland (MacPherson 117-124; Gimbutas).

The creativity-receptivity contrast is also evidenced in language, at least in those languages in which there is gender — so that activities that are perceived to be intrusive are masculine, while activities that are receptive are feminine. For example, words denoting thought, concept, analysis, are masculine, while those denoting imagination are feminine. In fact, the very word *imagination* is feminine in all Indo-European languages as well as in Hebrew; and in Latin, nouns resulting from abstractive processes (represented by the suffix *-io*) are feminine. It is as though receptivity, whether verbal, imaginative, or sexual, were always conceived along the model of the womb, the female void, and were therefore feminine (Neumann, *Art*, 182).[2] In so far as women are morphologically receptive, they symbolize receptivity.

Some contemporary research data (Gilligan; Dinnerstein; Grumet; Belenky; Fausto-Sterling 30; Paglia 23) seem to indicate a difference in cognitive orientation between men and women. Men seem to be prenatally (that is, not as a result of nurture) predisposed to know the world visually, while women seem equally predisposed to know it auditorily. This is connected with men's higher spatial ability and women's greater verbal fluency (LeVay 99 *ff.*). This is not a matter of exclusivity but of emphasis. Seeing and hearing, after all, are ways of knowing. Beyond mere neurology, to *see* is to envelope, penetrate, manipulate the world at a distance, while to hear is to receive the promptings of the world, also from a distance.

Thus we speak of a "penetrating gaze," and we help someone see by pointing (though we also speak of "taking it all in"). Knowing visually, as Sartre has shown, connotes a certain obtrusiveness, a quasi-sexual violation of the object by sight.

Figures of speech, sometimes vague and sometimes more precise, like that of the "unviolated depths" of nature suggest the idea of sexual intercourse more plainly. We speak of snatching away her veils from nature, of unveiling her (Cf. Schiller's *Veiled Image of Saïs*). Every investigation implies the idea of nudity which one brings out into the open by clearing the obstacles which cover it, just as Actaeon clears

> away the branches so that he can have a better view of Diana at her
> bath (Sartre, *Being*, 708).

As is clear from Sartre's example, the metaphors that convey visual knowing are male to the same extent to which they are visual.

On the other hand, hearing is a more receptive approach to knowing. The metaphors are telling: we *open* our ears; we *give* or *lend* our ears to speech; we *allow* ourselves to be addressed; and so forth (though we also speak of "eavesdropping"). Knowing, in this sense, connotes a quasi-sexual sense of being entered, of being penetrated, even raped, and the cavernous ear becomes an apt symbol of the female sex. Thus, in Apuleius's story, Psyche's entire encounter with Eros is an auditory one. Unseen servants guide her through the palace, bathe her, feed her, regale her with their songs, and Eros himself, when he visits her at night, is only heard (and, one assumes, touched), but never seen. Psyche's whole consciousness, then, is dominated by hearing. She is the prototype of the receptive consciousness, and is appropriately feminine. Here again the association of creativity with the masculine and of receptivity with the feminine is sustained.

In a related area, Josef Garai and Amram Scheinfeld have summarized data that show that "the male organism has an 'activity orientation' to the environment, whereas the female organism has a 'response orientation' to the environment" (269). They refer to Erikson's work, concluding with him that "boys tend to build tall structures, enjoy defiance of gravity . . . while girls build more horizontal structures with static interiors" (Garai and Scheinfeld 211).[3]

Phebe Cramer and Katherine Hogan also point out that, according to Erikson,

> the development of sexual identity depends in considerable part on the
> biological differences between the sexes. The sexual organs of boys
> are external, and they function by being erectable, by rising and falling,
> and by being actively intrusive and pushing out into the world. The
> sexual anatomy of females, however, is quite different. With the
> exception of the lips at the entrance to the vagina, the organs are
> entirely internal (Cramer and Hogan 151).

They go on to show how Erikson has "characterized the typical mode of behavior of boys in the phallic stage as being that of intrusiveness — pushing out into space — while for girls the typical mode is inclusiveness — incorporating or including activity within an enclosure" (Cramer and Hogan 151). According to Erikson, "if 'high' and 'low' are masculine variables, 'open' and 'closed' are feminine modalities" (Erikson, *Childhood*, 103-104).[4] Here again there is an association of creativity (intrusiveness) with masculinity, and of receptivity with femininity.

The womb does not merely symbolize the matrix of the world; it is also, as Jung put it, "the eternally sucking gorge of the void" (Jung, *Septem*, 383); that is, the receptive.

This view of the feminine is omnipresent. It appears in the *Odyssey* in Athena's guidance of Ulysses, Perseus, and Jason; in Dante's *Commedia* in Beatrice; in the knightly ideal of service to a lady not the knight's wife; in Cervantes's *Don Quixote* in the lure of Aldonza/Dulcinea; and more explicitly in Goethe's *Faust* in the figure of Gretchen/Margaret, clarified beyond doubt in the concluding words of Part II: "The Eternal Feminine/Draws us above!" It reappears in Hesse's *Narcissus and Goldmund* and in Pierre Teilhard de Chardin's poem "The Eternal Feminine," in which he speaks of "the magnetism of the Feminine" which draws by the lure of its purity to a vision in which "you may see with wonder how there unfolds, in the long web of my [the Feminine's] charms, the ever-living series of allurements — of forces that one after another have made themselves felt ever since the borderline of nothingness" (Teilhard, *Writings*, 194, 200, 202; de Lubac). As he puts it in another place, "woman stands before him [man] as the lure and symbol of the world" (Teilhard, *Human*, 34; Nichols 114-120).

The receptivity of the feminine is to be found also in the Nothingness of Buddhist contemplation and philosophy, the Void (*sûnyatâ*) or Womb that is the possibility of everything (*Astasâhasrikâ Prajñâpâramitâ* 18; Nâgârjuna, *Sûnyatâsaptati*; Macy 75-80). Similarly, it appears in the Aristotelian *materia* (*hyle*), the void of potentiality (*dynamis*) which Aristotle himself saw as "desiring" its corresponding form (*morphê*): "What desires the form is matter," he wrote, "as the female desires the male" (*Physics*, I.9 [192^a 22]).

It should be clear from the preceding that the association of creativity with the masculine and of receptivity with the feminine is not wanton or unfounded. Whether or not the hypothesis that sexism arises as male envy of female receptivity is substantiated, this connection stands, I think, on solid ground. The question, then, is, how can the hypothesis of the ground of sexism be proven? This is the task of the following chapters.

NOTES

1. Historically, this was not always the case. During Roman times as well as during the seventeenth and eighteenth centuries, a sexist bias crept into determinations of what was or was not biological maleness/femaleness. See Galen, *De Semine* 2, 1, in *Opera Omnia*, IV, 596. Gender remains fluid because of the many variants possible due to genes, hormones, chromosomes, and social milieu. See Blum.

2. The question whether gender is inherent to language or an artificial and inconsequential phenomenon is disputed among scholars. My own studies and multicultural linguistic experience make me lean toward the view that gender accrues to language from genderized experience. I am also convinced by Gaston Bachelard's analysis in *The Poetics of Reverie* (Boston: Beacon Press, 1971).

3. Speaking about the male pseudonyms employed by women writers, Joyce Carol Oates says that "Charlotte [Brontë]'s 'maleness' was very likely identified with the active, creative side of her personality, her 'femaleness' with the more passive" ("Success and the Pseudonymous Writer: Turning Over a New Self," *The New York Times Book Review*, December 6, 1987, p. 14). The word "passive" here is odious, but the association of maleness and the creative, on the one hand, and of femaleness and what I call the receptive, on the other, is well taken.

4. From a strictly psychoanalytic point of view, "the female is synonymous with the unconscious and the nonego, hence with darkness, nothingness, the void, the bottomless pit" (Neumann, *Origins*, 158).

Chapter 3

The *Hypo*- of the *Thesis*

It is one thing to connect creativity and receptivity with masculinity and femininity, respectively, and quite another to show that male envy of female receptivity exists and is one of the primary roots of sexism. After all, mere association proves nothing. What must be shown is that there is an active, positive avoidance and fear of receptivity on the part of men, and that this eventuates in sexist practices.

Two major facts, or congeries of facts, give rise to the hypothesis that sexism is connected with an unconscious wish to avoid reference to receptivity. The first one is *the exaggerated emphasis on creativity prevalent in societies the world over.* More will be said of this later in Chapters 4 and 5, but the following will give a brief inkling into the nature of the evidence.

To an impartial observer, it must seem odd that in most societies, especially Western, creativity is praised, emphasized, and "taught" almost to the neglect of everything else. Children, men, and women, are expected to be "creative" — that is, to produce and (by a queer quirk of language) to produce *original* works (Götz, "Defining Creativity," 297-298). No questions are asked about what it means to be creative; whether or not creativity can be taught; whether all kinds of creative endeavors should be fostered equally (*v.gr.*, production of weapons, of drugs, etc.); and so forth. And, of course, no mention is made of receptivity, the *fact* that creativity presupposes insight, and that insight requires a certain wonder, a certain receptivity.

Concomitantly, it has become transparent that for the past few thousand years the world has been ruled by men, and that men have imposed upon it what to them appeared to be appropriate modes of life — that is, creative ones. It is men, therefore, who have emphasized creativity at the expense of receptivity. In (at least partial) answer to the question why this should be so, the present hypothesis has been proposed.

The second fact is *the psychic experience of humankind as reflected in myth, religion, and fairy tale.* I am using myth in a very large sense, to include not only classical stories but also theology.

At first blush, the hypothesis that sexism is rooted in male envy of female receptivity and on an effort to cover up this lack may seem far-fetched. The objection may be raised right at the start that much, if not all, of what I am implying has no real foundation in the psychic experiences of men, and is therefore groundless. Men do not experience themselves as lacking receptivity or desiring it, nor do they admit to envy of women because of it.

But surely, the point of inquiry is, precisely, to set aside what a superficial consciousness avows and to look for the structures that may lie beneath the surface. Marion Woodman writes:

> I look at the dreams of women tyrannized by rapists, robbers, and dictators, and I look at the dreams of men threatened by sharks, wildcats, and witches. I see what each sex is projecting onto the other and I wonder how we exist together on the same planet, let alone in the same household or the same bed. What goes on inside goes on outside, or as Jung put it, "When an inner situation is not made conscious, it happens outside, as fate" [Jung, *Man* 185-186]. So long as we remain unconscious, our ambivalent feelings are imaged in our dreams. A woman who believes she loves her husband dreams she serves him an elegant dish of poisoned shrimp. A man who worships his wife dreams of driving a stake through her heart. Until the inner warfare is made conscious, the outer world will continue to be a battleground of the sexes (Woodman 145; Neumann, *Fear*, 165 *ff.*).

Only by such methods can one reinterpret the very superficiality of the ordinary consciousness, and lay hold of a more complex reality. To do this we must examine briefly the human psychic record as reflected in myth, religion, and fairy tale. We do this because, as Jung put it, "myths go back to the primitive storyteller and his dreams" (Jung, *Man*, 90; Bettelheim 36). In other words, myths go back to the time when stories were told to account for practices that were being instituted or that were being interpreted (or reinterpreted). Myths incarnate the (sub)consciousness of people "at the beginning." This examination must be very restricted in nature, as it inquires merely into some myths, those in which negative attitudes toward women's receptivity are detected, and primarily (almost exclusively) into Western myths and fairy tales.

My hypothesis is structurally the following: If stories, myths, and fairy tales reveal in their symbolisms a male anxiety about, fear of, and envy of women's receptivity, one explanation is the repression of affects connected with the object of the anxiety. Freud asserted that "every affect belonging to an emotional impulse, whatever its kind, is transformed, if it is repressed, into anxiety" (Freud, "The 'Uncanny,'" XVII, 241). The hidden anxiety is revealed in dreams or in stories. My hypothesis seeks to trace the anxiety through the story, and is obviously based on Freud's general approach to psychic data.

I am following here only the structure of Freud's approach. I do not wish to imply by this any agreement with the psychosexual content of his theories. This is not an original approach on my part. It has been followed by several writers, Bruno Bettelheim among them, and it is based on Freud's own psychoanalysis of literature, art, and myths.

The point is, if anxiety is present in determinate instances, it must be because of certain experiences charged with feeling which, because of a perceived emotional impact, are repressed. Repressed feelings appear in dreams and stories. Analysis of the stories and the anxiety that generated them, therefore, should yield some inkling of the emotion and what impacted on it.

Further, as Freud suggested and exemplified in his application of dream analysis to works of the creative imagination, it is possible to analyze myths and fairy tales for their latent content. This kind of psychological analysis does not at all detract from the meanings of such stories discovered at other levels. Myths can be read in many ways, and none of them are denied; but the purpose here is to use them as gateways to the unconscious fears and apprehensions of humankind through the centuries.

THE DATA FROM MYTHOLOGY

In world mythology, women's receptivity is often symbolized by the unconscious itself (Neumann, *Origins* 158), and therefore the latter's symbols are the very symbols of the former. The unconscious has been connected with the feminine since time immemorial. A clear case is Ereshkigal, goddess of the "underworld." This connection also appears in, among other things, the recurring belief that women are especially suited to gain access to the unconscious and to "the forces of darkness."

In all civilizations, through to our own times, primarily women have been mediums. They have been the sibyls, oracles, and witches, the "knowing" ones whose special lore became associated with the Prince of Darkness under Christianity (Christian theologians, it would seem, could not justify a *woman*'s "knowing" except through deviltry). It was to such a woman that Saul went at Endor in an effort to converse with the deceased Samuel (*I Samuel* 28:3-25). The Pithya at Delphi was a woman; so was the celebrated sibyl of Cumae, and so still is the priestly *Mãe de Santo* who presides at a Brazilian *candomblé* (sacred precinct for the syncretistic rites of Bahía). Umã, daughter of the Snowy Heights (*himavati*), taught Indra and the other gods the secret that the Self is Brahman (*Kena Up.*, 3.1-4.3). Diotima, needless to say, was a woman, and so were Deborah, Medea, Circe, Hildegard, Julian of Norwich, Mother Ann "the Christ," and Madame Blavatsky.

The unconscious, symbol of the female receptive, is not always benign. It is often the monster that threatens the rational order of the ego. It is the whale that swallows Jonah and that destroys Ahab. It is the labyrinth, unending in its twists and turns, harboring the horrifying Minotaur. It is the dragons that guard the damsels of Mediaeval legend, and that are feminine in Chinese mythology. It is the sea serpent that curls round the desolate rock where Andromeda pines. It is Leviathan rising from the depths against YHWH. It is Mephistopheles in *Faust*, termed "part of that power which, willing evil, accomplishes good" (*Faust*, I, 1335-1336). More specifically feminine, the unconscious is Tiamat

(Hebrew *tehom*), the chaotic watery depths tamed by YHWH (*Gen.* 1:2) or conquered by Marduk.

It should be noted that dragons guard unmarried, that is, "virgin," damsels. One way of reading this is to see the dragon as symbolic of the omnivorous, terrifying Id, untouchable and forbidding to men, who needs must "conquer" it (that is, defeat the dragon). Until that happens, the sexuality of the virgin is terrifying, like a dragon. The dragon, then, may be seen also as the projection of men's fears of female sexuality, especially sexuality pure and simple (the sexuality of the "virgin," that is, of woman before she becomes mother).

THE DESCENT OF INANNA

In a very special way, the unconscious is Ereshkigal, Queen of the Underworld, older sister of Inanna (Queen of Heaven and Earth, Goddess of Love, Morning and Evening Star). The myth of the descent of Inanna to the underworld was inscribed probably around 1750 B.C.E. in tablets which were discovered in the ruins of Nippur (Wolkstein and Kramer 127).

> From the Great Above
>   she opened her ear to the Great Below.
> From the Great Above
>   the goddess opened her ear to the Great Below.
> From the Great Above
>   Inanna opened her ear to the Great Below.
>
> My Lady abandoned heaven and earth
>   to descend to the underworld.
> Inanna abandoned heaven and earth
>   to descend to the underworld.
> She abandoned her office of holy priestess
>   to descend to the underworld (Wolkstein and Kramer 52).

As Inanna enters the underworld, the symbols of her power, her crown, her jewels, and eventually her robe, are removed. Her queries are met with the cryptic remark: "Quiet Inanna, the ways of the underworld are perfect. They may not be questioned" (58). Finally,

> Naked and bowed low,
>   Inanna entered the throne room.
> Ereshkigal rose from the throne.
> Inanna started toward the throne.
> . . . . .
> Then Ereshkigal
>   fastened on Inanna the eye of death.
> She spoke against her the word of wrath.
> She uttered against her the cry of guilt.
>
> She struck her.

Inanna was turned into a corpse,
   a piece of rotting meat,
   and was hung from a hook on the wall (60).

Inanna, the young woman who reigns above the heavens, has descended into
an "underworld" unknown to her. There, in darkness and dirt, reigns her sister
Ereshkigal, the enthroned Id: instinct, desire, greed, rage, hatred, coldness,
"and desperate loneliness" (158). Ereshkigal represents both the outer world of
unexplored and threatening experience as well as the inner world of Inanna's
(and everyone's) unconscious; what we are, too, but fail to acknowledge; our
"shadow," as Jung called it; those qualities and impulses we deny in ourselves
yet so easily spot in other people (Frantz 168). This darkness is threatening to
all, but it proved especially so to men as they slowly came to power thousands
of years ago. Edward Whitmont writes (135): "For the emerging patriarchal
consciousness the Ereshkigal aspect of existence is utterly terrifying. It is . . .
avoided or at least controlled as much as possible."

One of the reasons why Ereshkigal is threatening and terrifying to men is
that she is active. Receptivity is not passive. An overwhelming proof of this
are the thousands of Tantric statues in Hindu temples. The void, the unconscious, sucks us in (or "draws us above": there is no real difference). As
Diane Wolkstein puts it, Ereshkigal's "one great craving is for her own sexual
satisfaction . . . . [Her] sexuality is compulsive, insatiable, and without
relationship to offspring" (Wolkstein and Kramer 158). It is, in other words,
pure (sexual) receptivity.

Even Inanna's sexuality is terrifying because it, too, is active (Whitmont
134). Like her sister, she craves, commands, lusts, enjoys her men in sex and
in power:

My vulva, the horn,
o · · · ·
Who will plow my vulva?
Who will plow my high field?
Who will plow my wet ground?
· · · · ·
Who will station the ox there?
Who will plow my vulva? (Wolkstein and Kramer 37).

Tantalizing as this may seem, it is also threatening to the emerging male
consciousness, and many a man pays dearly for congress with "the Star." As
Dumuzi, Inanna's consort, bewails, "My shepherd's crook [phallus?] has
disappeared!" (75).

THE EPIC OF GILGAMESH

The *Epic of Gilgamesh*, too, may be read as the record of a man's journey
of discovery of the feminine in general, as well as of his own femininity.

In the beginning, Gilgamesh is depicted as the violator of young virgins and married women: "His lust leaves no virgin to her lover, neither the warrior's daughter nor the wife of the noble" (Sandars 62). The people suffer, but not in silence. In fact, it is their complaint to the gods about the unrestrained lust of their king that convinces them that something must be done. The result is the creation of Enkidu, whose *raison d'être* is, therefore, to lead Gilgamesh to a new understanding of sexuality and to a different kind of sexual behavior.

That the reason for Enkidu's coming is the enlightenment of Gilgamesh in the ways of the feminine is clear from the whole tenor of the narrative. To begin with, Enkidu is to be Gilgamesh's "second self" (Sandars 62). He is created by the goddess Aruru, and even though he is strong and rough, "he had long hair like a woman's," and "it waved like the hair of Nisaba, the goddess of corn" (Sandars 63).

While this new creation is taking place, Gilgamesh has two dreams. In the first one he sees a meteor (identified later as Enkidu) fall down from heaven. Gilgamesh tries to lift it, but he cannot; and yet he is attracted to it as to a woman. He narrates the dream to his mother, the goddess Ninsun, who admits that Enkidu will be a goad and a spur to Gilgamesh to search himself; that he will be drawn to him as though to a woman; and that he will love him "as a woman" (Sandars 66). The same interpretation is given to Gilgamesh's second dream, in which he sees an axe (identified as Enkidu), and is drawn to it "powerfully like love of a woman" (Sandars 67).

When Enkidu comes into the life of Gilgamesh, the two embrace "and their friendship was sealed" (Sandars 69). Strong though he is, Enkidu represents the more feminine aspect of Gilgamesh, perhaps even his *anima*. He listens to women with great care; he allows himself to be taken by the hand and to be led by the harlot; he does as she tells him. When he confronts Gilgamesh it is to protect women from his violent and intemperate lust (Sandars 67-69); and when finally he is at death's door, he is unable to curse the harlot. On the contrary, he blesses her and promises her a bright future (Sandars 90-91).

Enkidu comes into Gilgamesh's life at night, as Gilgamesh is on his way to assuage his lust with another young bride (Sandars 69). Enkidu blocks his way. They fight; neither wins, and they become fast friends.

From this moment onwards, Gilgamesh is on a journey to the other side of his own self, the feminine. But he still yearns to conquer. Hence the proposed journey to the Mountain of Cedars guarded by the giant Humbaba (whose name means "Hugeness"). The Cedars of the mountain represent woman, since wood is frequently a female symbol.[1]

A change begins to take place. Woman is no longer a mere prey to his wanton lust. Sex with her is an achievement that must be won. The Mountain of Cedars represents his new attitude. The Mountain is his *Venusberg*, and he approaches it (her) with the same bravado of old.

The Mountain is the mature woman, more difficult to approach than the young, inexperienced, defenseless maidens he had claimed. This is a new stage in his approach to the feminine. Humbaba is the monster/dragon that invariably keeps guard over the gardens (the goddess's precincts). Such guardians must be conquered, defeated, or tricked. Joseph Campbell mentions the dream of a married gentleman: he wanted to enter a wonderful garden, but in front of it was a watchman who prevented entry. Campbell comments: "The powers that watch at the boundary are dangerous; to deal with them is risky" (*Hero*, 82). Not that Gilgamesh has not abused married women before. But he had done so as King, not as man, and therefore his had not been a real confrontation with the feminine. The approach to the Mountain of Cedars reveals a new understanding of woman as mysterious; her sex is dangerous.

With the machismo of old he pretends everything is fine. But the boasts Gilgamesh utters are denied by his unconscious: his dreams are of fear. While he shouts, "Forward, there is nothing to fear!" (Sandars 71), his first dream is frightening: "Ah, my friend, what a dream I have had! Terror and confusion . . ." (Sandars 77-78). His second dream is even more terrifying: he sees himself caught "in a deep gorge of the mountain" (Sandars 78), when suddenly the Mountain falls, overshadowing him. Twice he mentions his feet, a primitive phallic symbol (Freud, "Three Contributions," in Brill 567; Campbell, *Hero*, 79). In the context of the meaning of Humbaba, "the Huge," it is fair to suppose some feeling of sexual inadequacy, such as would be experienced in the presence of a god like Priapus. His third dream is equally frightful, for in it he feels the earth heave and the winds sigh and roar, and the clouds "rained down death" (Sandars 79).

Clearly, Gilgamesh is subconsciously frightened by his impending encounter with full-blown, mature, female sexuality. Raping virgins, brides, and house-wives is easy considering his power: he is the king, and his pleasure is the thing. But Enkidu has been sent to enlighten him, to help him discover the full extent of the feminine. And discovering the feminine entails discovering the awesome power of female sexuality.

Gilgamesh conquers his fear, invades the Mountain, captures Humbaba, and in a throwback to the wantonness of his earlier days, turns a deaf ear to Humbaba's pleas for mercy and kills him (Sandars 82-83).

With the wantonness return his old fears. When glorious Ishtar (Inanna) invites him to be her lover, Gilgamesh refuses (as Picus rejected Circe, though for different reasons): "Your lovers have found you like a brazier which smolders in the cold . . . a castle which crushes the garrison. . . . You have loved the lion . . . you have loved the stallion . . . you have loved the shepherd . . . the gardener. . . . He was changed to a blind mole deep in the earth, one whose desire is always beyond his reach" (Sandars 86-87).

In a sense, the Mountain of Cedars is symbolic of Ishtar, the mature goddess of love, Queen of Heaven and Earth. Having initially conquered his fear of her, Gilgamesh is still not ready to approach her full sexuality. When Ishtar loves, she is in command; her desires come first, her satisfaction (not that of her consorts) is the rule. Gilgamesh the king will have none of that.

Gilgamesh's quest for unity within himself, for the integration of the feminine in his own life, fails. The unmerciful killing of Humbaba is followed by the destruction of "the Bull of Heaven" (Sandars 88). The bull, who from antiquity had symbolized the Goddess as nurturant and protecting, is slaughtered and quartered to spite Ishtar. The result? "One of the two must die" (Sandars 89) — that is, the feminine is sacrificed to the wanton violence of revenge and abuse; it must disappear. Enkidu is stricken by illness, and Gilgamesh weeps for him, "bitterly moaning like a woman mourning" (Sandars 94); and when Enkidu lies, finally, dead, Gilgamesh lays a veil upon his face "as one veils the bride" (Sandars 95).

Under the guidance of Enkidu, Gilgamesh has changed. He has at least acknowledged the feminine as more than prey, as more than an object of his lust. He has overcome (at least temporarily or partially) his fear of mature female sexuality, but his victory is not complete. The subconscious fears remain, and the preoccupation with victory and prowess stifle the completion of his inner search. He is still afraid of death, not merely the death that overtakes us all as mortals, but the death he must submit to in the entrails of the feminine (that is, by becoming a "mole"). He is afraid of being cut down to size by the cavernous mouth of the womb. He can only enter in anger, as he tells Siduri: "I will break in your door and burst in your gate" (Sandars 101). Siduri's advice, "'Make your wife happy in your embrace; for this too is the lot of man'" (Sandars 102), goes unheeded. All he can think of is his own immortality.

Thus, his quest for an understanding of the feminine, within himself as well as outside, is not fully successful, just as his quest for immortality also fails at the last minute. But some change has taken place. "While the Gilgamesh who dies at the end of the epic is a greatly changed, greatly enlarged human being from the totally selfish despot who opened it, he is, quite appropriately still not 'whole,' still not 'perfect.' This gives the narrative its base of realism" (Absher 28).

Seductive femininity, sexual receptivity, symbolized here by the Mountain, is a threat to the patriarch. But why? Is it only because of its activity and independence?

THE FAUSTIAN MOTHERS

Thousands of years later Faust, too, is horrified when Mephistopheles, messenger and minion of the underworld, suggests that the only way to obtain Helen is to go to "the Mothers."

> FAUST: Mothers!   6217
> MEPHISTOPHELES: Do you fear?
> FAUST: The Mothers! Mothers! What a strange sound
>   that is.
> MEPHISTOPHELES: Strange it is. Goddesses to men unknown,
>   Whom we are loath to name or own.
>   . . . .
> FAUST: Whither the way?

MEPHISTOPHELES: No way! To the Unexplorable
    Never to be explored; to the Unseekable,
    Not to be sought.
   . . . .
    Naught will you see in that vast Void afar   6246
    Nor hear your footstep when it's pressed,
    Nor find firm ground where you can rest.
   . . . .

FAUST: Into the Void I'm sent.
   . . . .
    Come, let us fathom it, whatever may befall.
    In this your Naught I hope to find my All!
   . . . .

MEPHISTOPHELES: Descend, then! I might also tell you, Soar! 6275
    It's all the same. Escape from the Existent
    To phantoms' unbound realms far distant!

What is so frightening in all this? Why should Faust shudder? We know what troubles him. Mephistopheles explains it unwittingly:

MEPHISTOPHELES: Formation, Transformation   6287
    Eternal Mind's eternal re-creation.

Becoming; change; that is the meaning (Jantz 59). The receptive is the empty potentiality into which every creature must enter in order to be reborn or changed. The empty womb symbolizes it. It is threatening because, while we "know" that nothing can be reborn unless it dies first (*John* 3:1-10), it is risky to give up what we are for the sake of what we *may* be.

    Is this, too, perhaps an apprehension lurking behind Hamlet's dealings with Ophelia and with his own mother? In his adolescence he had loved Ophelia, but that was before the matter of the Queen, his mother's, incest was brought up by the Ghost. After the revelation, the Queen is no longer just his mother; she is a woman who lusted for Claudius even while Hamlet's father lived. Her womb is not just mothering — the acceptable thing; it is receptive, sexual, active, threatening. Perhaps Ophelia, too, appears suddenly in a new light: she is woman, and her sex, too, threatens. It was easy to love her with the innocence of youth, but now she is better dead or in a nunnery. The Queen, too, must be unsexed: she must refuse to sleep with Claudius and withstand his sexual overtures. And while this may be interpreted as Hamlet's concern for propriety, the respect due his dead father, and solicitude for the spiritual well-being of his mother — after all, incest is a sin — the anxiety about her lust cannot be discounted outright. Similarly, while the spurning of Ophelia must be seen as part of his plot to avenge the murder of his father, the sexual dimension seems implicit in his thoughts, to say the least.

    Men prefer not to look too closely at the dark abysses of the feminine where things dissolve, disappear, are even destroyed. That is why men accept more readily the life-giving properties of the Goddess (Whitmont 135-136). Men hail woman as mother, not as virgin (that is, as self-possessed, as beholden to no one) (Weideger 56); and to make sure that this virginal mystery will remain distant, men turn it into the sugary notion of the chaste virgin (that is, the woman untouched by men) or demean it into that of the temple prostitute. The point is to avoid confronting the unformed darkness of possibility which is experienced as threatening in the fact that it connotes risk. Thus the effort in ancient times was to obliterate as much as possible the symbol of transformation. The men in power saw to it. As Whitmont put it (136), "Henceforth woman was to renounce the threatening power of her 'dark moon' side, be chaste and humble and cease tempting man with lust and passion, lest the abysmal power of the feminine dissolve his firm will and render him over helplessly into the maelstrom of transformation." This unapproachability of virginity is shown sometimes by the inability of young men to obtain the ladies of their dreams, as in the story "The Old Woman in the Wood." The maiden is approached daily by the king's son; not directly, but in the shape of a dove, which he assumes once a day; for he has been turned into a tree by a wicked Old Witch. As long as the maiden is seen as virgin, as mere openness, her sex frightens and impedes approach. Only when the maiden, willing to marry (that is, to cease being a virgin), has stolen the plain wedding ring from the Old Witch, does he feel capable of approaching her. This happens when she, unaware of the curse placed on the king's son, leans against the tree he is, and slowly feels him become human and tender: "As she thus stood, it seemed just as if the tree was soft and pliant, and was letting its branches down. And suddenly the branches twined around her, and were two arms, and when she looked around, the tree was a handsome man, who embraced and kissed her heartily" (*Grimm's Fairy Tales*, 560).

It is to be noted that it is not only the feminine "without" that is threatening and to be avoided or covered up; the feminine "within," the *anima*, the unconscious, may portend, too, the risk of potentiality and change to which men must surrender if they are to change and grow (Whitmont 138).

No change can take place without some destruction. What is must dissolve into what is not before it can emerge again as what is. To fall into that receptacle is forever the tantalizing yet frightening task of becoming. Woman reminds man of all this because she is the receptive *par excellence*, while man lacks any distinctive physiological reminder of possibility.

THE FLOOD

In his book *The Divine Woman*, Edward Schafer writes:

The *Tao* is no abstract entity . . . but rather a great mother, an eternal womb from which emerge all of the particular entities that populate this ephemeral world. . . . Part of the imagery which attempts to flesh out this imprecise entity is aqueous, and an inspection of the whole concatenation leads one easily enough to the construction of a primitive, female, all-enveloping ocean of fertility, something like the Babylonian goddess Tiamat. . . . Ishtar, a mother goddess and "daughter of the ocean stream," with Isis, a fertility and river goddess, ruler of the Nile's flood, with Aphrodite . . . and with the Virgin Mary herself who, to the Gnostics, was "of the sea" (Schafer 33).

He could have added that for Roman Catholics the Virgin is still *Stella Maris*, "Star of the Sea," and that *tohu wa bohu*, the "chaotic waters" of *Genesis*, is linguistically connected with Tiamat.

All beginnings are feminine. As beginnings, they are indeterminate, openended, endowed with a liquid amorphousness that can be terrifying. Form seems safe and solid, even when it is so only in illusion; formlessness is frightening as the deep waters of the sea are frightening. It is not so much that the sea contains monsters as that it is profound, shapeless, unfathomable. Hence, the feminine, too, is daunting and forbidding.

Water is the feminine substance *par excellence*, something well known to the ancients. In China, in the summer of 813 C.E., there was a flood in the T'ang Empire. The monarch, Li Ch'un (Hsien Tsung), was persuaded that it was the result of an excess of *yin*, the feminine principle. On July 21 he forthwith expelled from his palace two hundred wagonloads of superfluous women, since they represented *yin* (metaphysical water) in human form (Schafer 6).

Flood myths are almost universal. According to Michael Grant, they "occur in thirty-four out of a specimen group of fifty among the world's mythologies" (Grant 351). Many see these stories as "hero myths," that is, myths centered around heroic figures — Ziusudra, Utnapishtim, Noah, Deucalion, Kung Kung; others see them as stories of re-creation, the gods being angry with their original design for people and then deciding to obliterate it and start anew. "The uproar of mankind is intolerable," Enlil complains to the Sumerian gods (Sandars 108), while in Greece

> Jove was witness from his lofty throne
> Of all this evil, and groaned as he remembered
> The wicked revels of Lycaon's table,
> The latest guilt, a story still unknown
> To the high gods. In awful indignation
> He summoned them to council . . .
> And then he spoke in outrage:
> "... a race
> Must be destroyed, the race of men. I swear it!"
> (Ovid, *Metamorphoses*, I.163 *ff.*)

Genesis 6:5-7 also echoes the outrage: "When YHWH saw how great was man's wickedness on earth, and how every scheme that his mind devised was nothing but evil all the time, YHWH regretted that he had made man on earth, and there was sorrow in his heart. And YHWH said, 'I will blot out from the earth the men that I created.'"

The various interpretations of the flood stories have their value; complex myths need complex study. But it is clear that the waters that destroy the earth and its inhabitants — the *feminine* waters — are tumultuous, chaotic, fearful, and that a lesson is thus conveyed: it is better to serve the (male) gods than be visited by the (female) waters of another flood; it is better to step on solid ground than be steeped in the liquescent nothingness of floods. Deucalion says to Pyrrah:

> Look! Of all the lands
> To East or West, we two, we two alone
> Are all the population. Ocean holds
> Everything else; our foothold, our assurance,
> Are small as they can be.
> (Ovid, *Metamorphoses*, I.353 *ff.*)

Men want that reassurance, small though it be, and prefer it to the truth, the truth that Utnapishtim reveals to Gilgamesh: "There is no permanence" (Sandars 106).

HERAKLES

The "Second Labor" of Herakles has him battling and then killing the Lernaean Hydra. All the connections here are feminine: Hydra (water), born to Typhon and Echidne; Lerna, a seaside region flanked by the rivers Pontinus and Amymone. The place was sacred to Dionysus and, especially, to Demeter, whose Lernaean Mysteries were celebrated there. The Hydra, reportedly, had a dog-like body and between seven and ten thousand heads: accounts vary. One of the heads was immortal. Herakles severed the immortal head and, with the help of Iolaus, cut the others and cauterized the wounds, so they would not sprout again.

It seems clear that the references here are to the colleges of priestesses — water-priestesses — residing in Lerna. Their numbers varied, but obviously there were efforts to curtail them and even to destroy them and to eliminate their fertility rites (the "mysteries") altogether. Not everyone agreed with Cicero's later judgment that the mysteries, especially those at Eleusis, have taught us "the fundamentals of life" (*principia vitae*) and "the basis not only for living joyfully but also for dying with a better hope" (*De Legibus*, 2.14.36). Robert Graves comments: "Heracles's destruction of the Hydra seems to record a historical event: the attempted suppression of the Lernaean fertility rites. But new priestesses always appeared in the plane-tree grove . . . until the Achaeans, or perhaps the Dorians, burned it down" (Graves, II, 110).

But the reason for the elimination of the colleges of priestesses was not solely the imposition of the worship of male gods by the Achaeans or Dorians upon goddess-worshiping people: the goddess's powers were feared, something hinted at by the description of the Hydra as a terrifying monster. Here again it is the fear of the feminine that powers the destructive actions of the man Herakles.

THE AMAZONS

Stories about powerful, even warlike women, abound in ancient literature, even as late as the sixteenth century C.E. The stories may refer to pockets of matriarchal societies, remnants from pre-Indo-European times. Such pockets appear to have existed in Ireland, England, northern Africa, around the Black Se ҙ. India, China, and even South America. The Greeks referred also to the island of Lemnos, visited by Jason and the Argonauts, as a dwelling place for women only. Argos itself seems to have favored the right of women to be independent and unattached. This is reflected in the myth of the fifty daughters of Danaüs, who refused to marry, and when obliged to, killed their young husbands on their wedding night (all except Hypermnestra, who spared the life of her Lynceus).

But such quests for independence were rare during Greek times, and headed for extinction, a point made, perhaps, by the kind of punishment the Danaïds were given. In the underworld, they had to fill water jars riddled with holes, so the water poured out and the task was never accomplished. Maybe the male storytellers understood that in an increasingly patriarchal world, woman-centered societies would soon disappear altogether.

The most "famous" of these groups were the Amazons. If it is true that Amazons existed in various parts of the world, and if their way of life has been accurately rendered (a dubious proposition, since the chroniclers were men), it is understandable why they were feared. It is said that Amazon tribes mated indiscriminately once a year with the males of surrounding peoples. The female offspring were kept, the male ones killed, maimed, retained as slaves, or returned to their fathers.

Medusa, a Gorgon, was one of the queens of the African Amazons that lived probably around present-day Algeria, Morocco, and Tunisia. If the custom of her tribe was the maiming of men, no wonder she was invested by men with the horrible traits she has brought down in legend. Scythian women, too, are said to have used their moon-sickles for castration as well as for war and agriculture; a long-handled version of their sharp instrument became known as the scythe.

Armed, such women inspired fear in their male enemies, but many of the myths about the Amazons contain the theme that men can fall in love with them after they have been disarmed and rendered powerless. This point is important regardless of whether or not the Amazons were in fact as they were depicted in myth, legend, and historical records. The subconscious motif of the Amazon and similar myths is that women can negate men, eliminate them (Chesler 108-113) — in other words, that men are afraid of them, and that men will approach them only when they have been "neutralized" and/or rendered harmless; perhaps even killed. According to one story, the Amazons attacked Athens (Plutarch, "Life of Theseus"), and some, under Queen Penthesileia, came to the aid of Priam during the Trojan war.

> That day the beating of full many a heart,
> Trojan and Argive, was for ever stilled,

> While roared the battle around them, while the fury
> Of Penthesileia fainted not nor failed;
> But as amid long ridges of lone hills
> A lioness, stealing down a deep ravine,
> Springs on the kine with lightning leap, athirst
> For blood wherein her fierce heart revelleth;
> So on the Danaans leapt the warrior-maid.
> And they, their souls were cowed; backward they shrank,
> And fast she followed, as a towering surge
> Chases across the thunder-booming sea
> A flying bark, whose white sails strain beneath
> The wind's wild buffeting, and all the air
> Maddens with roaring, as the rollers crash
> On a black foreland looming on the lee
> Where long reefs fringe the surf-tormented shores.
> So chased she, and so dashed the ranks asunder
> Triumphant souled (Quintus Smyrn., *Posthomerica*, I.312-325).

Achilles confronted her, and angered by her boasts and her exploits, he thrust his unerring spear and pierced Penthesileia above her right breast. Angry still, he thrust again so powerfully that the iron went through her horse

> Even as man in haste to sup might pierce
> Flesh with the spit, above the glowing hearth
> To roast it (*Posthomerica*, I.612).

The spear went clear through the animal, and it pierced Penthesileia also; and so

> Face down she lay
> On the long spear outgasping her last breath.
> Stretched upon that fleet horse as on a couch
> (*Posthomerica*, I.623).

As Penthesileia lay dying, Achilles vaunted her for her bravery, which seemed recklessness to him. He drew the spear from her and from her mount while they gasped their last breath, and violently plucked the helmet from her head, exposing her great beauty, and prompting a cry of pity from his lips. Some say he then raped her inert body (that is, her "safe" body) (Graves, II, 313),[2] drawn perhaps by her great beauty, or as a magic rite to appease her vengeful ghost. For the killing of a woman was certain to be avenged by the Furies. Later, Achilles is said to have made expiatory sacrifices at Lesbos, and to have been finally purified by Ulysses. It is, of course, significant that such an appeasement would have been rape. The story reveals both the fear of the female even in death, and her degradation by the patriarchal heroes.

In China, the stories were of swordswomen, "virtuous, brave, beautiful, and skilled in the martial arts" (Beh 122), who may still be seen in some present-day martial arts films. One of them was the warrior woman, Fa Mu Lan, a girl who took her father's place in the battle against injustice. But in China, as in the West, patriarchy, too, moved on relentlessly, and such women of power and courage had to be tamed. Maxine Hong Kingston wonders: "Perhaps women were once so dangerous that they had to have their feet bound" (Hong Kingston 19; Beh 125).

SECRET FEARS

But there is more. Faust's quest for the Mothers to get Helen is reminiscent of Perseus's search for strength from the Gray-haired Graeae, to kill Medusa (Ovid, *Metamorphoses*, IV. 773-777). Medusa was one of the Gorgons, the only mortal one, a creature with wings and with live snakes for hair; so horrible that whoever looked at her was turned to stone. According to Freud, Medusa's snaky head represents the female genitals crowned by pubic hair, frightful for men to behold because they hold up for them the fear of castration (Freud, "Medusa's Head," XVIII, 273; Whitmont 135; Paglia 16).

Fear of castration is part of the Freudian system, but there is here a pre-requisite unmentioned by Freud. This is the fear of the female receptive (vulva) that can alone negate the male creative (phallus). For the womb exists before it is entered. Brandishing his sword (a symbolic phallus), Perseus asserts himself. He is still "whole," and he will obliterate the face before it can maim him, before it can receive him, swallow him; but more pertinently, before it can remind him that its mouth is something he will never have.

The problem is that women cannot but remind men of their own male inadequacy. To be a woman is to have something a man will never have. To be a woman is, therefore, to be threatening to men, to be a *femme fatale*, such as Delilah was to Samson, Jael to Sisera, Judith to Holofernes, and Salome to John the Baptist.

We have a similar meaning in the story of Artemis (Diana) and Actaeon (Ovid, *Metamorphoses*, III.138-252); it conveys the awe inspired by the nakedness of the feminine. Having come unexpectedly upon Artemis naked in the woods, Actaeon is "disabled" (as John Ruskin, by his own account, was "disabled" at the sight of his bride's pubic hair) — he is turned into a stag and becomes the prey of his own hunting dogs.

The story of King Kong's demise reflects the common version of woman as *femme fatale*. To look upon the face of feminine beauty (as an apocryphal Arabian proverb informs us at the start of the film), is to lose one's male power and, in effect, to be like one dead. That is exactly what happens to Kong. His interest — a clear sexual interest in Ann Darrow — renders him impotent and, eventually, paves the way for his destruction (Rubinstein 111; Morgan 71-72).

For centuries, and in many cultures, sexual intercourse was believed to sap a man's powers. Implicitly, of course, woman was the culprit, the "sucker." This view was not always presented directly; often it appeared in symbolic form in the treatment of hair. For example, it is said that Samson derived his physical strength from his hair. But it is obvious from the account (*Judges* 13-16) that Samson's prowess was sexual as well as physical. His demise comes about ostensibly when the secret of his physical strength is found (namely, his long hair), which is shorn treacherously by Delilah. But there is also an indication here that it is sexual promiscuity that causes his capture and death. Cutting the hair, then, symbolizes *both* some form of emasculation as well as control of aggressivity (Leach). Either way woman's sex is man's downfall (Rubinstein 111).

As the tales of the Lorelei, the Rusalka, the Sirens, the Dragon Spirits of China, and others show, men feel threatened by the questioning that women's very being is. From this point of view the many stories of rape, starting with the rapes by Zeus, Poseidon, Hades, Achilles, and Tereus, seem to imply that rapes are revenges by men for the treatment they feared at the hands of the Mother Goddess. The Goddess's love destroyed her many mates, for it is not possible to be loved by the Goddess and be healthy afterward, as Gilgamesh discovered, and as happened to Anchises, on Mount Ida, through the wiles of Aphrodite.

Many subsequent stories display a rising fear of women, and opposition to their overtures of love and sexuality. Gilgamesh refuses Ishtar, Picus refuses Circe, Odysseus repulses both Calypso and Circe, Hippolytus scorns sexual Aphrodite while worshipping chaste Artemis, and also refuses the amorous overtures of Phaedra (much as Joseph would those of Potiphar's wife). These same points are made also in several fairy tales.

In "The Story of the Youth Who Went Forth to Learn What Fear Was," the young man's fear of the female openness (Medusa's "head" glimpsed, perhaps surreptitiously, in his naked mother) leads him to repress his own sexual desires. He is unable to tremble or shudder (i.e., to be "aroused").[3] This is an unusual state, since most people do shudder when confronted with frightful (and sexual) experiences. Anxiety supervenes, and the young man leaves home in order to learn how to shudder, for it is impossible for him to do so at home, a point picked up by Freud in his analysis of the Oedipus Complex.

The young man wants to learn how to *shudder*. This point is worth noting. Even though the story's title states that his purpose is to learn what fear is, it is clear from the story itself that his incapacity relates to trembling, not to fear. Perhaps there is an implication that fear and shuddering are synonymous, since all who truly fear experience a concomitant shudder. So it is possible to read the story as implying that the suppression of desire extends to the fear of the desired (otherwise how could he have consented to marry?), and therefore to a divorce of trembling from fear — that is, a separation between sex and orgasm. In fact, as belief had it, no conception could take place without "shuddering." What prevents him from fearing ghosts and other ghastly sights is that repression of his fear of sexuality has rendered him immune to the shudder of fear in general. The *dénouement* occurs when the young man learns to "shudder" in his marital bed through a clever diversionary or distracting (*dedifferentiating!*) trick performed by the maid (Bettelheim 281).

In another example more directly related to male fears of being found out to be lacking wombs (i.e., receptivity), Bluebeard, the suave murderer, would hand his young brides the keys of all the rooms of his mansion, with explicit instructions not to open one, the one where the corpses of all previous wives were held. To cover up what is in the small room, he gives her all manner of distractions: jewels, furniture, tapestries, gold and silver. Once the little room is opened and the corpses of the slain former wives are found, revenge begins in full: the little key is spotted with blood that cannot be cleansed or rinsed; she must be found out, and his revenge will be unstoppable, for anyone, especially any woman who discovers his secret, must pay the prize with his or her life. How accurately does this reflect the male revenge for the discovery of his impotence, of the fact that his little room is full of corpses, that he no longer has a little room, that he has no room at all.

That was Bluebeard's secret, and no one violating it could live. Similarly, in the "Fitcher's Bird," the wizard would leave his latest kidnap victim with all the keys to the house, and with the prohibition to enter a particular room; and in the story "Faithful John," there is a room that must not be opened by the young king, for it contains the picture of the princess of the Golden Dwelling. The reason is that, if he sees her picture, the king will fall violently in love with her. The princess's picture, therefore, is bewitching. Put differently, there is a terrifying as well as an alluring aspect to the first encounter with a young woman: love is the allure; the terrifying part is sexuality, which induces fear in the young king. Without Faithful John's help he will not succeed in the process of maturing.

These stories, comments Bettelheim (300), "present in the most extreme form the motif that as a test of trustworthiness, the female must not inquire into the secrets of the male." What secrets are those — his lack of special receptivity, his wish to have "his own room," his envy of the female's womb, and his fear that if what he claims as his own room is opened it will be found *filled* (that is, a nonroom) — except that he will be found to have no womb?

NOTES

1. The association is: *madera* (Spanish: wood) ——> *madeira* (Portug.: wood) ——> *materia* (Latin: matter) ——> *mater* (Latin: mother). Here we have the combination of Mother and Nature, of which more will be said in Chapter 4.

2. The main source for the rape story is the *Aethiopis* of Arctinus, as summarized by Proclus, *Epicorum Graecorum Fragmenta*, ed. G. Kinkel. Apollodorus, *Epitome*, V.1, and Quintus Smyrnaeus, *Posthomerica*, I.625 *ff.*, state simply that Achilles "loved her." The verb used is *èraô*, which implies a passionate sensual (sexual?) love. Graves calls the story "characteristically homeric" (II, 319), and assumes it may have been censored from the *Iliad* by an editor during Peisistratus's tenure.

3. "Shudder" is equated with orgasm. See Nicolas Venette, *Conjugal Love; or the Pleasures of the Marriage Bed Considered in Several Lectures on Human Generation* (London, 1750), p. 41.

Chapter 4

Creativity *Über Alles*

The contention of this book is that much of sexism manifests itself as envy of female receptivity (rather than of female creativity — that is, of motherhood). I have shown in the preceding chapter how this envy and, at the same time, fear of female receptivity appear at the unconscious level in myths and fairy tales. I must now demonstrate that the avoidance of receptivity and the emphasis on its opposite, creativity, appear, too, in many religious beliefs and social practices, eventually constituting a fundamental aspect of the social malaise we call sexism.

WOMB ENVY

The notion of "penis envy" introduced by Freud is well known. According to it, women see themselves as imperfect men, castrated, incomplete, partial males, who, in Margaret Mead's words, "can never be as important as he is because they lack his full equipment" (Mead 81). But the reverse view also is plausible. Gregory Zilboorg makes this point in cogent terms:

> If one is to adhere for a moment to the traditional idiom and speak in terms of superiority and inferiority, "the idea that the female is naturally and really the superior sex seems incredible, and only the most liberal and emancipated minds, possessed of a large store of biological information, are capable of realizing it." Therefore, if the discussion of the biological superiority of one of the sexes and of the discomfort of conscious and unconscious inferiority of the other is to be continued, I must submit that it was man who perceived himself biological inferior, and it was this sense of inferiority and concomitant hostility that led to the phenomenon of couvade — a magic, compulsion-neurotic, hostile identification with the mother. *It is out of this identification with the mother that psychological fatherhood is achieved.* There may very well be not a little surprise at the paradoxical conclusion to which this study seems to have led, but it seems almost inevitable: The sense of paternity is essentially a feminine attribute ultimately acquired by the human male in his attempt to keep his mastery of the female more secure and less disquieting in light of the periodic demonstration of female superiority by way of having children. I am inclined to think that it is not

penis envy on the part of the woman, but womb envy on the part of the man, that is psychogenetically older and therefore more fundamental (Zilboorg 289-290).

Zilboorg has in mind here envy of the womb as creative. But the same psychological mechanism would apply if men envied the womb as receptive. What if the most obvious fact in the development of children is not the awareness (prereflective, of course), sooner or later, that the penis is missing in one sex, but that the vagina is missing in one sex — and the sudden comprehension by the boy that he will never have one (Erikson, *Identity*, 267, 274)? It would not be far-fetched to conclude, as Karen Horney does, that the impact of such a realization is perhaps most clearly reflected "in the unconscious of the male psyche in the boy's intense envy of motherhood" (Horney 10; Mead 104; Miller 46; Stannard 325). Envy of motherhood there may, indeed, be. But more fundamentally, this is envy of the womb *per se*, of the empty openness of the feminine.

INITIATION

That this awareness-cum-envy exists is manifested by certain aspects of the initiation rites of boys. Mircea Eliade remarks how in many rites circumcision was followed by subincision in a symbolic effort to give the initiate a female sex organ (Eliade 25; Sanday 86). The overall intention is to render the boy androgynous in the belief that he stands a better chance of becoming a man if he first becomes a totality, a male-female, as the original humans are thought to have been (Eliade 26; Stannard 290-291). As part of the initiation, the boys are also dressed up as women, are referred to in feminine terms, and even perform chores that ordinarily are reserved for women.

No parallel rite exists for girls. Even where clitoridectomy or scarification are practiced in a ritual corresponding to circumcision, the intent seems to be sexual readiness rather than a masculinization of the girl.

A woman does not become more powerful or authoritative, but more creative, more alive, more ontologically real. . . . The pattern of female initiation is thus one of growth or magnification, an expansion of powers, capabilities, experiences. The magnification is accomplished by gradually endowing the initiand with symbolic items that make of her a woman, and beyond this a cosmic being. These items can be concrete, such as clothing or jewelry, or they can be nonmaterial in nature, such as songs chanted to the woman-to-be, myths repeated in her presence, scars or paintings placed upon her body (Lincoln 103-104; Woodman 17-18).

She appears to be complete, androgynous. The boy, on the other hand, needs to capture for himself, at least symbolically, what she possesses naturally — the receptivity of the womb.

OBSCENITY AND POSSIBILITY

According to Sartre, "the obscenity of the feminine sex is that of everything which 'gapes open.' It is an *appeal to being* as all holes are," since woman's condition is seen primarily as "'in the form of a hole'" (Sartre, *Being*, 752). For Sartre, the vulva is not obscene — that is, repugnant — because it is filthy, but because its openness is a threat; it symbolizes the openness of possibility, but possibility itself is threatening because it entails risk. From this one may infer that castration is not so much the fear of losing the penis as the fear of being turned into a quasi-woman — an impossibility — and therefore the fear of having to deal with one's (lack of) receptivity. Male impotence, thus, is not just inability to get it up; rather, it is inability to plug the hole. We fear what we lack; we embark on creativity to protect ourselves from our lack, and so the images we create in literature and the arts bear witness to "a persistent male terror of women's sexual awakening."[1]

Men have no such reminder of possibility. Hence the effort to cover up the evidence: through emphasis on virginity before marriage, through sex and pregnancy in marriage. The hole must be kept padlocked, and Pandora's opening her "jar" is seen as the cause of all evil in the world. This explains partially the Mediaeval chastity belt, and in the contemporary world, the even more bestial practices of some African countries by which the newborn girl's labia are scraped and sealed until marriage; later unsealed for intercourse; and often resealed after motherhood (Daly 153-177; Dworkin, *Intercourse*, 192-194).

THE BODY POLITIC

Maxine Sheets-Johnstone quotes researchers Ford and Beach to the effect that

> exposure of the genitals by the receptive female seems to be an almost universal form of sexual invitation throughout the mammalian scale. Descriptions of the mating patterns characteristic of various subhuman primates . . . [show] the ubiquitousness of feminine exposure. . . . The female ape or monkey characteristically invites intercourse by turning her back to the male and bending sharply forward at the hips, thus calling attention to her sexual parts (56),

a position depicted artistically by much nineteenth century painting of women (Dijkstra) and reproduced, with clear invitational overtones, by recent *Pepsi* TV commercials.

This kind of sexual signaling remained possible as long as primates were quadrupedal. Bipedality, however, when it became persistent among hominids, had the effect of shifting the placement of female genitalia slightly to the front and, at the same time, away from easy visual inspection. Bipedality, in other words, made female genitalia hidden, *and therefore* necessitated a radical change in female sexual signaling behavior (Sheets-Johnstone 60-61; Nadeau 26-28). This change took place concomitantly with the disappearance of oestrus.

Two major consequences flowed from these two physiological changes. To begin with, the disappearance of oestrus meant that females could be sexually active and/or receptive all the time. It meant also that they were *perceived* by males as always available, because they no longer possessed distinctive behaviors to signal their readiness and/or desire. In time, females came to be assumed to lack sexual desire, since they seemed to lack the natural powers of sexual expression. Consequently, females were perceived as being simply open and available year-round. From this still current Western and essentially male point of view, human females were assumed to invite copulation — to be available for it — simply by being there: they themselves were an invitation (Sheets-Johnstone 62, 67).

Second, year-round availability was construed as year-round receptivity, and while from a sexual point of view this may have appeared as an encouragement for males to avail themselves of what was always at their disposal, it also had the effect of making males constantly aware of what they lacked, namely, a distinctive receptivity. From this point of view year-round receptivity meant a year-round reminder, and, consequently, a year-round threat. Males came to perceive the perennially available females as murmuring, by their very existence, "I *am* what you have not got." From this perspective, sexual (ab)use of the year-round available female may be seen not only as wanton male sexual domination of the female through intercourse and rape, but, equally at least, as a spiteful and at least momentary obliteration of the gap that perennially reminds him that "he ain't got it."

In brief, the development of year-round availability threw into prominence female physiological receptivity. While the corporeal sign (vulva) became hidden, the *fact* of year-round receptivity was thrown into prominence, and this prominence had the double effect of bringing to the fore that whereby females are threatening to males *and* of giving males an opportunity to think themselves primary in the control of sexuality and of females: females were perceived as available to men regardless of their readiness and/or willingness. Men could, therefore, more wantonly indulge their sexual pleasure while subduing, controlling, and obliterating that which threatened them.

In some respects year-round receptivity became the ground for new behaviors designed to place the males in control of sex, not merely to assuage their sexual instincts, but equally in order to obliterate the receptivity precisely by controlling it through intercourse — even rape (which by definition is not concerned with *giving* pleasure because it judges women as incapable or unworthy of it). In other words, the available receptivity was "used" not merely for the satisfaction of male sexual urge, but, equally at least, for the (temporary) obliteration of the receptivity men were jealous of and threatened by.

Here a further question arises. Given the hiddenness of female genitalia due to persistent bipedality and the consequent lack of specific female signaling of sexual availability or desire, are there substitute behaviors for that lost natural signaling? The answer is yes. To cite but one example, Sheets-Johnstone (57 *ff.*) suggests that various researches among human and nonhuman primates have demonstrated that when a female sits with her legs spread, "her genitals become quasi-visible and accessible" (58). Such a posture would normally be taken as a substitute signaling behavior — except for the fact that in just about all societies, females are not permitted to sit with their legs spread wide. This prohibition is achieved either by clothing or by mores, or by both, and is another example of the control of female sexuality achieved by males. Obviously, it is also indicative of men's unwillingness to be reminded of female receptivity.

There are, of course, other sexual signalling behaviors as well as behaviors indicative of female receptivity *per se*, and even though the latter are not as significant, perhaps, as the more sexual ones, nevertheless they enhance our understanding of this issue of male attitude toward female receptivity.

Nadine Gordimer, in her short story "Home," describes a scene in which Teresa, the female protagonist of the story, receives her husband with welcoming hands "palm up." The gesture is distinctive. Women, generally, signal their receptivity by greeting with extended arms and hands palm up. The corresponding male gesture of domination is palm down, and men seem to have difficulty holding hands with others (especially females) with hands palm up. Of course, as with so many other differences between men and women, this distinction is gender specific though not gender exclusive, since women will approach others with their hands palm down when the intent of the gesture is clearly to control or dominate, and some men, at least in some situations, will have no difficulty being receptive and will signal their readiness by holding or offering their hands palm up. Parenthetically, handshakes are neutral, hand meeting hand in neither a receiving nor a controlling position.

None of this should be surprising considering that, as Ray Birdwhistell puts it, humans "and probably other weakly dimorphic species necessarily organize much of gender display and recognition at the level of position, movement, and expression" (52), and "palm up" (P/\) is a specific and identifiable kineme (374) that seems to have a similarity of meaning in many cultures irrespective of sexual intent. Thus, for example, the universal hand position for "imposing or laying on of hands," as in ordination, cure, or blessing, is done with hands palm down. So is the swearing in hand position when the oath is taken upon a book such as the Bible. Such positions imply the transmission or the exercise of power and are still predominantly male. On the other hand, offering gestures, either to the divinities in prayer or to fellow humans, and imprecatory gestures, such as requests for pardon and compassion, characteristically occur with the hands palm up, and in most instances typify the female either as praying priestess or as weak and submissive petitioner. But even priests, for example, while they offer prayers during mass, are directed to hold their arms with hands palm up. Typically, too, the position of the hands (*asana*), either in the lap or on the knees of the squatting Hindu yogi or Buddhist ascetic, is always palm up. A combination of both is to be found in the prescribed gestures of ecstatic dancing dervishes, whose right hand is turned palm up in a gesture of reception while the left hand is turned palm down in a gesture of transmission of the divine grace.

The general significance of the hand palm up as implying receptivity, and its more frequent association with women, has its roots in the natural openness and receptivity of the female reproductive system. In Mark Johnson's words, "concrete bodily experience not only constrains 'input' to the metaphorical projections but also the nature of the projections themselves, that is, the kinds of mappings that can occur across domains" (p.xv). As Sheets-Johnstone puts it, "clearly, one's concept of power and one's concepts of possible deployment of power arise on the ground of the body one is . . . the body *simpliciter* [that is, abstracted from sociocultural accretions] is the source of individual 'I can's'" (48). But the female body *simpliciter* can receive in ways the male body cannot. Therefore the connection is more natural to women than to men, especially because now that the vagina (natural symbol of receptivity) is hidden, other symbolic gestures and/or behaviors must develop to symbolize receptivity, not just in a sexual sense (such as legs widely spread might be), but in a more general sense. Hands palm up is one such gesture. By extension, the supine female's legs-spread position (*body*, rather than *palm*, up) is the one "preferred" by males in sexual intercourse (the male's position turning the *body*, rather than the *palm*, down). Traditionally, and to signify the dominating nature of this behavior, this sexual position was termed "the missionary position," and since men were in charge of determining what was and what was not lawful, this dominating position was read into law in many states in America, to the point where it was deemed "illegal" for a woman to bend over the man in sexual intercourse, and to do so without being caught was thought to be deviant (D'Emilio and Freedman 83).

CONCUBINAGE

Concubinage has been another way of placing the sexuality of women at the service of men. In China, for example, some emperors had as many as one hundred royal concubines, who played a backgammon-like game daily in order to decide who would share the emperor's bed for the night — only to have the emperor sometimes ignore the winner and follow his fancy. While lesser noblemen could not match this number, the richer they were, the more concubines they kept. The poor, of course, were monogamous.

The rationale for the system was complex and subtle. Men, commentators noted, remain sexually active into old age, while women are thought to lose their attractiveness by forty. Hence the need to stock the harem with younger beauties. Moreover, it was felt that one woman, or even a few, could not perform the various tasks expected of women: wife, lover, mother, dry nurse, maid, literate companion, musician, and so forth. On the contrary, "the more women, the richer the content of life — *for the men, that is*" (Mitamura 82; emphasis mine). As a Chinese put it, the system is like a tea set. Who would think of having only one teacup for one teapot? In the West, this very attitude is echoed by Creon's comment to Haemon, "There will be other furrows for your plough!" (*Antigone* 569).

INTERCOURSE

Andrea Dworkin claims (*Intercourse*, 97; *contra* Paglia 19) that intercourse has a metaphysical dimension. This means that intercourse is symbolic, but symbolic of what? "Male desire in reality is a sexual recognition of female as female," Dworkin writes (*Intercourse*, 98); intercourse is the empirical proof that *she is*, and that therefore he can use her. I take this to mean that what men seek in intercourse is the use of the space that women are; that they seek a receptivity that characterizes women and that, they think, (metaphysically) women represent or symbolize. Intercourse, actual penetration, is the empirical verification of the metaphysical quest.

But why would men seek this metaphysical receptivity incarnate in women? Dworkin's answer is, so that they can *use* women. Why? *I* answer: to cover up, to plug the hole, the symbol of male lack.

Men want what women have; what women are. And to have it they plunge, desperately, into her hole, not merely to obliterate the evidence of their own lack, but to *seem*, briefly, "like women," their organ sunk temporarily beyond sight. The motivation is not sexual; it is metaphysical.

Obviously, this is not the motivation for all intercourse. Use and abuse, *pace* Dworkin (*Intercourse*, 122; Paglia 2), are *not* synonymous, in language or in fact.[2] My concern is with abuse, with the violent occupation of the space that women are, an experience I believe Dworkin chronicles very well.

RAPE

My concern is with rape. One first-person account will serve as illustration. The story is that of an eighteen-year-old college freshman, and it happened in 1981:

> The rapist attacked me from behind. He and I fought in the open. I screamed. I punched and scratched him with my nails, but he eventually got me on the ground. With a knife in one hand and the other so tight around my throat I couldn't breathe, he made it clear that he would kill me if I didn't cooperate. He dragged me into an abandoned tunnel. He stripped me and repeatedly raped me on top of broken beer bottles. He kept me prisoner for two hours. He urinated on me, he called me every obscenity, and he forced me to perform oral sex (Sebold 16).

This is a story of violence against a young woman. That is what rape is, violence against women (by which I do not mean to deny the existence of male rape). But the focus here is the investigation of this violence against women that uses sex as its primary weapon.

It is generally agreed today that the rape of women is not primarily motivated by sexual desire as much as by hatred of women.[3] In ancient times, this is very clear in the rape of Lucretia by Sextus. Today, the literature and the documentaries on rape like to show the connection between early childhood experiences of the rapist and his subsequent rapist behavior. Rejections or beatings by mothers or significant females, jealousy or envy of favors accorded other males, losses, humiliations, and similar experiences are said to create the psychological conditions likely to lead to hatred of women and to rape. But why *rape*? Hatred can be vented in many ways; violence is multifaceted, and in many rapes, the sexual aspect is really secondary. So why the sexual aspect at all? We need a metaphysical motive: rape singles out for outrage what is distinctive in women, their receptive systems. It is not as mothers women are raped, but as women. Typically, the gods, from Enlil, Amon-Re, and YHWH to Zeus and Hades, ravished young maidens, and the "right of the first night" was exercised upon virgins.

A similar pattern is to be found, I think, connecting pornography and sexism. The controversy continues to rage about the *causal* link between pornography and rape. Studies are inconclusive, but the tendency has been to see pornography as a psycho-causal root of rape. But pornography and rape (or generally violence against women) may be connected in a different way, namely, by reference to the same hatred of the womb, a hatred that leads to violence (in the case of rape) and to ridicule and prurience (in the case of pornography). In the former, the hatred eventuates in anger, while in the latter it results in the cowardly depiction of the violation men feel afraid of performing (but would if they could). Rape is the crime of the violent; pornography, that of the weak. Both are patriarchal; that is, they have their origin (*archê*) in men's hatred of what women *are*.

Bram Dijkstra shows clearly how by painting women as weak and languorous, and by describing them as passive — and by suggesting that all this was "natural" — the implication arose that "it was only natural to take her by force, since by her behavior she seemed forever to be pleading to be taken by force" (Dijkstra 100). "It was thus perfectly all right to force a woman. She could not help her initial resistance to a man's advances, after all, given her basic lack of knowledge about sexual matters. But as soon as she had been initiated, even if the means had been force, her very nature, her very longing for completion, would make her cleave to her master with ever greater intensity" (Dijkstra 103).

Thus, it was seen as natural that women should be beaten by their men; in fact, it was even thought that it was natural for women to love to be beaten, for in that they showed their subordination to their husbands or lovers. Nana, in Emile Zola's novel, finds herself momentarily dazed the first time Fontan slaps her, but by the next morning she has rationalized the violence: "She loved him too much. Why, it was even nice getting a slap, provided it came from him" (Zola 251). In fact, violence was such a natural thing that it enhanced a woman's health, and when slaps became as regular in Nana's life "as the tick-tock of a clock," she thrived: "By dint of being beaten, Nana became as supple as fine linen; her skin grew delicate, all pink and white, so soft to the touch and pleasing to the eye that she looked more beautiful than ever" (Zola 265).

The same idea is conveyed by Mark Twain in "Eve's Diary." After the

Fall, Eve asks herself why she loves Adam. She runs through a number of reasons — his brightness, his gracious and considerate ways, his industry, his education, his chivalry — and rejects them all.

> Then why is it that I love him? *Merely because he is masculine, I think.*
> At bottom he is good, and I love him for that, but I could love him without it. If he should beat me and abuse me, I should go on loving him. I know it. It is a matter of sex, I think (Twain 1125).

PURITANISM

Far too many sexual encounters take place today in the context of what Rollo May calls "puritanism with a small *p*" (May 45). Victorians, May points out, had difficulty dealing openly with sex, so they "made love"; we, on the other hand, have difficulty dealing with love, so we "have sex"; or, for men, in a more warlike pose, we "score," "conquer," or "perform." Sexual intercourse, in other words, is engaged in mostly to satisfy lust. In sex today, love takes a holiday.

The contrast with Victorian Puritanism is helpful, I think, but it masks another reality. This is the fact that for most of recorded history, much sex has been devoid of love. The oppression of women is proof of this. For the most part, intercourse has satisfied lust, and the lust of the man, for the most part. Men have been in control, and they have used women to satisfy their desires. An interesting example is the *Kâma Sûtra* of Vâtsyâyana, where most of the poses would leave a woman unstirred. The control of women in society and culture is in no small way connected with their domination in sex (Dworkin, *Intercourse*, 63-64).

Women are enslaved because social mores countenance the use of some people as means to other people's pleasure. As Tolstoy put it, "the enslavement of woman lies simply in the fact that people [men] desire, and think it good, to avail themselves of her as a tool of enjoyment."[4] The culmination of the enjoyment is, of course, intercourse, which requires the penetration of the woman's cavity, the invasion of her receptive space. Viewed from this perspective, women are desired for the enjoyment their "space" provides. Put differently (but, I think, still truthfully), women are desired because the use of their receptivity is enjoyable. By joy I do not mean only orgasm. I mean, primarily, the (unconscious) joy of possessing what one lacks.

FEMININITY AND THE WORLD

"Maleness and femaleness," Edward Whitmont writes, "are archetypal forces. They constitute different ways of relating to life, to the world. . . . The repression of femininity, therefore, affects mankind's relation to the cosmos" (Whitmont 123). Given the association of creativity with maleness and of receptivity with femaleness, this means that sexism represents an effort to put down the receptive ways of approaching the world: wonder, caring, contemplation, and the imagination.   Examples abound.   One thinks of Colonel Faversham, in *The Four Feathers*, determined to drum army bravado into the sensitive soul of his young son.   One thinks of the millions of boys whose tears were stopped by the taunt, "Don't be like a girl!" (In my nursery school class, where boys and girls sat on opposite sides, boys who didn't know the answer to a question were punished by being made to sit among the girls.)   One thinks of the ways the artistic processes have lacked support through the ages, while the products of art were grabbed and hoarded by the rich and powerful.   One thinks of the verbal praises of contemplation and the factual preference for action, a preference that is subtly detectable even among the Western religious orders themselves, which have slowly moved from contemplation to action over the past eight hundred years.

FEMININITY AND MATTER/NATURE

It must be remembered that the last two thousand years have seen a blending of the Western attitudes toward women with the *materia* the Gnostics pronounced evil.   A similar merging took place in India between matter (*prakriti*) and the Goddess of pre-Aryan religion, but without pejorative connotation (Bharati 205).

Since the advent of patriarchy several thousand years ago, women have been relegated to the background, to household chores and domestic cares.   As in most, if not all ancient traditions, this was the case, too, in Israel. Christianity inherited this attitude despite Jesus's reform efforts, for it is clear that one of the distinctive characteristics of Jesus's message and actions was that a *sine quâ non* for entering the Kingdom, or for the Kingdom to come, was the equality of the sexes.   The oneness explicitly recommended and prayed for by Jesus (*John* 17:11 and 21; *Mt* 19:6) includes equality of the sexes, as is clear from the letters of St. Paul (*Rom.* 3:22 and 10:12; *I Cor.* 12:13; *Ephes.* 2:15; *Col.* 3:11; *Galat.* 3:28) and, overwhelmingly, in the apocryphal literature (*v. gr.*, *Gospel of Thomas* 22; *2 Clement.* 12).

But during its formative years, Christianity was influenced by ancient dualistic beliefs originating in Persia.   According to these, spirit was good, and matter was evil.   Matter, especially in its fleshly, sensual aspects (*sarx*), was despised.   It had to be controlled and eventually transcended, but in the meantime it was to be thought of as despicable, and treated likewise.

Slowly, however, this lowly *materia*, including the essential possible of Aristotle, became identified with woman, the eternal void. Contact with matter, which for the Gnostics was defiling, became the defiling contact with women (*Revel.* 14:4).   The identification was not far-fetched: *Genesis* implied it,[5] and Aristotle himself had made it, as was pointed above.   But this identification carried a new twist, the aspersion of evil.   Women were seen as created by the evil Demiurge in the same way as matter was proclaimed created by the evil Auhra-Mazda, or it/she was a remnant of Sophia's concupiscence.[6]

Thus, the evil of matter, even of matter the possible, was transposed to woman the void, and the symbols of woman were also changed into symbols of evil. For example, paradise, the garden (*shal*), originally the garden-womb of the Goddess Mari (*shal-Mari*; *Shalimar*), becomes *sheol*, "the pit," an unpleasant hell or underworld. The womb-garden becomes the womb-tomb; the good womb becomes the bad womb, "the pit," and so, too, does the possessor become evil.

Henceforward woman's sensualness (her materiality, one might say) became the paradigm of evil. Tertullian called woman "the devil's gate" (*De Cultu Femin.* I.1). Potentiality became incompleteness, and woman was the incomplete *par excellence*, an imperfect male, as the Christian tradition pronounced her. The following passage from Otto Weininger's *Sex and Character* (*ca.* 1906) is revealing:

> Women have no existence and no essence; they are not, they are nothing. Mankind occurs as male or female, as something or nothing. Woman has no share in ontological reality, no relation to the thing-in-itself, which, in the deepest interpretation, is the absolute, is God. Man, in his highest form, the genius, has such a relation, and for him the absolute is either the conception of the higher worth of existence, in which case he is a philosopher; or it is the wonderful fairyland of dreams, the kingdom of absolute beauty, and then he is an artist. But both views mean the same. Woman has no relation to the idea, she neither affirms nor denies it; she is neither moral nor anti-moral; mathematically speaking she has no sign; she is purposeless, neither good nor bad, neither angel nor devil, never egotistical (and therefore has often been said to be altruistic); she is as non-moral as she is non-logical. But all existence is moral and logical existence. So woman has no existence (Weininger 286, 220; antecedents in Roussel and Moreau).

At about the same time, Miguel de Unamuno's novel, *Amor y pedagogía* (1902), gives expression essentially to the same feelings. For Avito Carrascal, the novel's protagonist, "genius must necessarily be masculine" (51). Against his better judgment and the careful plans he had laid out, he falls in love with Marina, and rationalizes his "fall" this way: "'There is no matter without form. I will be art, reflection, conscience, form; she, Marina, will be nature, instinct, lack of conscience, matter. What nature! What instinct! What matter! Above all, what matter! . . . What matter! I shall work it, as water works the earth; I will plough it, will give it form; I will be its artificer'" (59). God alone is perfect and male, pure Act, with no admixture of potency (that is, of matter or of femininity).

Much of the despising of woman comes in the Western tradition from the despising of matter, that is, of potency, of the void, of the receptive. As Robert Faricy puts it, "When Copernicus took Mother Earth from the centre of the universe and replaced it with the masculine sun, nature and women took a fall. With the scientific revolution, nature was perceived not as an ordered cosmos but as an unruly and disordered field for man to conquer, dominate, and use.

And nature was generally perceived as female, as feminine" (Faricy 38).

Seeing woman as nature, or part of nature, had the effect, too, of justifying men's conquering of women in the same way as the conquest of nature had been justified by reference to the *Genesis* account.   Darwinism, when used as justification for placing humankind in opposition to nature, had the same effect. As the embodiment of nature, woman was seen as being at war with man, who therefore was as justified in subduing her as he was in conquering nature (Dijkstra 237).

FEMININITY AND TANTRA

Pre-Aryan worship in India seems to have centered around the Mother Goddess.   The invading Indo-Europeans, however, were strongly patriarchal, and their gods were male.   Nevertheless, their domination of India did not completely obliterate local cults.   Over the years new syncretistic forms of worship and new ideologies appeared which reflected, though in a new garb, the old religious priorities.   Thus Shâmkhya came to conceive the basic elements of the universe as consciousness (*purusha*) and nature (*prakriti*), which it classed male and female respectively.   Peculiarly, however, it considered the male passive and the female active (a sort of *natura naturans*).   In later Tantrism, the passivity of the male was maintained in Shiva, and the activity of the female in Shakti.   In fact, in ordinary language *shakti* means power, or strength.   The old preeminence of the Goddess can be discovered in the belief that it is through the union of Shiva and Shakti in sexual intercourse that he is empowered to be Lord (Bharati 205, 212).   Thus the female power reasserts itself.

However, the *practice* (*sâdhanâ*) of Tantra is another matter.   While the participants, man (*sâdhaka*) and woman (*shakti*), are supposed to reenact in ritual sexual intercourse (*maithuna*) the union of the primordial couple, Shiva-Shakti, the man is in command.   Even though the ritual is supposed to be removed from ordinary sexual pleasure (*Brihad-aranyâka Upanishad* vi.4.3), it is the man's orgasm and ejaculation that assume importance.   His meditation is supposed to be sustained throughout their lying together; his prayer is to the Goddess; and he must constantly repeat the appropriate *mantra*.   But the culmination of the ritual occurs as he ejaculates with the words, "I, the exulting one . . . offer this . . .: *Svâhâ!*" (Vaidyarâj, *Vâmamârga* 111).   Thus, the ritual, while theologically centered around the sacramental transmission of power (*kundalinî*) to the male, ends up in his sexual gratification.   Woman, once again, is used.   Her receptivity, acknowledged even in the *Kâma Sûtra* (2.1), becomes subservient to male pleasure.

CHRISTIANITY AND MISOGYNY

The whole issue of receptivity and the feminine has been a target of the Western religious tradition, especially of Christianity.   Here one must be careful, for it is not a matter of discussing the general misogyny of Western religion but only of those aspects of it which directly concern the receptive.

Opposition to women's learning did not appear with Christianity. Judaism had restrained it, and even the Greeks expressed unease at a woman's learning, as Euripides attests (*Hippolytus* 640). Still, Socrates disdained not his learning from Diotima (Plato, *Symp.* 201); Sappho's poetry rivaled Pindar's; Leontion's books were praised by Cicero for their "neat Attic style" (*De Natura Deor.* I.33.93); and not a few *hetairai* were said to have run symposia that rivaled the French salons of the eighteenth century.

Beginning with St. Paul, women were forbidden to speak in church (*1 Tim.* 2:11-12). This prohibition was extended to study: learning, especially philosophy and theology, were outside their realm of competence (Stannard 47-62). This interdict was maintained until recent times, and still continues in the refusal to let women become priests. True, it was softened by Aquinas and others, and was attacked by writers such as Cristina de Pisan. True, too, there were exceptions: Macrina, Hildegard von Bingen, Marie de France, Jean Bodin, and the many women mystics who committed their visions to writing. But generally, they were not accorded importance, and in the case of women mystics, they had to be certified orthodox by the male hierarchy. Clearly, women were supposed to assume only the passive role of hearers.

This subordinate role was reflected in the social activities of women. While women performed just about every possible task, from physician, professor, and queen to maid, stable hand, and prostitute, the expectation was that they would remain within their place, subservient to the men in their lives. Even their names were changed into their husbands' after marriage (Stannard). Departures from this inferior state were looked askance, and often punished. Because of her extraordinary learning, Hypatia, though not a Christian, was savagely murdered by fanatic Christian monks under the leadership of Deacon Peter and with (at least) the consent of St. Cyril, Patriarch of Alexandria (Gibbon, II. 47). Joan of Arc was condemned to death, essentially, because she wore men's dress and refused to give it up; and thousands of women were tortured and put to death as witches because they presumed to "know" (medical arts, usually) without having attended the universities. To the mentality of the times, any knowledge not certified by the male establishment could come only from the devil.

The model for this passive, submissive woman, was the Virgin Mary, the woman whose personality was completely subsumed in that of her Son, and who defined herself as the handmaid of the Lord. It is not irrelevant to note that the ascendancy of the worship of the Virgin coincided with the rise in the systematic exclusion of women from the universities and with the persecution of witches.

The submission of women to men extended even to sexual intercourse. Women were expected to be "under" the man, and courtesans in France were called "*les grandes horizontales*." This is the so-called "missionary position" which in the United States was legislated and enforced by the male constabulary until very recently. In fact, according to nineteenth-century male expectations, women in sex were not even supposed to move.

None of this would be comprehensible without an underground ideology that justified and enjoined the lower status of women.   There is, of course, the example of the Virgin Mary, preached and eulogized in treatise after treatise. There is, also, the Pauline mandate that women be subordinate to their husbands in imitation of the Church's submission to Christ (*1 Cor.* 11:3; *Ephes.* 5:22-33). But there is, further, the subtle view that makes receptivity synonymous with passivity, and turns passivity into a sign of weakness, a "womanish" character attribute proper only of inferior creatures like women.

According to the theologians of the Middle Ages, woman contributes nothing to procreation.   She is purely a vessel, a receptacle, and her fluids are merely potency (*materia*) to be "actualized" and "informed" by the male sperm (*forma*). Activity counts, passivity does not; receptivity is needed, but creativity is better. In fact, creativity is good, even religiously good.   Using as justification the *agraphon* of Jesus, "It is more blessed to give than to receive" (*Acts* 20:35), the religious tradition downgraded acceptance and openness, while praising giving and action.

A case in point is Shel Silverstein's beguiling story *The Giving Tree*. Briefly, this is the story of a relationship between a boy and a tree.   The tree (*f.*) gives the boy shade, climbing opportunities, fruits to be sold for profit, wood to build a house, a trunk to construct a boat, and finally a stump to sit on. Through the many years of the relationship the self-sacrificing tree (*f.*) is happy.

Behind the seeming innocence of the story lies a powerful message of subordination.   The tree is female and is nature.   The boy is the eternal Adam "on top," whose dominance is "natural."   This is good "'kiddie porn'" (Dunnsmith-Burger 8), a parable of the female expected to sacrifice herself on demand, to accept gladly her subservience to the male even to the point of extinction, to entertain abuse at the hands of the male as an exercise of *his* right over her, and to find her happiness in this kind of masochistic existence.   To boys and girls, the story conveys the subtle message — "subliminal pro-fanations" (Dunnsmith-Burger 9) — that

> a "successful" love relationship requires docility on the part of its female member, not equality, not mutuality . . . that male (Boy) rules female (Tree) . . . that she "is happy" with her position and function in relation to the he. She even invites him to sit on her . . . [that] it is better to be a boy than a girl. . . . And look what boys can do to trees, girl trees. Anything they want. And the girls like it; it makes them "happy" (Dunnsmith-Burger 9-10).

Not merely is woman inferior and subservient, she is also a temptress. This role had been assigned to women even in ancient times; witness the story of Samson and Delilah; the stories of mermaids, nymphs, and water sprites; and the legend of the Sirens luring Ulysses away from his appointed goal.   But the *Genesis* story of the Fall casts Eve in the role of temptress, and the theme becomes endemic.   From Tertullian down, women are seen as a danger to the spirituality of men.   As stated in the medieval "Story of the Grail," "To steal away the minds and hearts of men, God made of her a wonder, and never before or since has He made her equal" (Loomis 38).

No wonder it is so difficult today to make the (otherwise obvious) case that receptivity (whether in art, vision, learning, or sex) is not passive, and that it is necessary and good; certainly as good and necessary as creativity.

SUBJECTIVITY AND FEMININITY

There has been a tendency to put down the subjective point of view, and whether this is due to the association of women with subjectivity (i.e., arbitrariness) or of subjectivity with women, I do not know.   Simone de Beauvoir (xv) writes: "Woman has ovaries, a uterus; these peculiarities imprison her in her subjectivity, circumscribe her within the limits of her own nature." This means, I take it, that there is a connection between female receptivity and subjectivity.   Men, on the other hand, are thought (by men) to be preeminently objective, and to be able to apprehend things as they are.

The point is not whether complete objectivity is possible.   Obviously it is not, and Kant, Goethe, and Heisenberg have reminded us of this.   As Jeane Piaget has demonstrated (6), the human approach to the world always involves (though with varying emphases) two invariant functions, *assimilation* (i.e., the incorporation of data into the mind's framework) and *accommodation* (i.e., the mind's adjustment to the massiveness and irreducibility of the data).   In being assimilative the mind is subjective (i.e., subject-centered); in being accommodative, it is objective (i.e., object-centered).   The point is that subjectivity should have been aligned with the presence of inner spaces or receptacles such as women have, and that in being condemned to an inferior knowing status, women should be termed subjective.

Put differently, the point is that here again there is a clear effort to value more the kind of knowing men are supposed to be capable of, and to put down women's receptive/subjective knowing.   This is apparent in the schooling system, where disciplines with a more "subjective" bent (such as literature and the arts) are considered "soft" and "effeminate," while those with a more "objective" orientation (generally math and the sciences) are considered "tough."   It is so in the schools, too, where modes of thought that are analytic, inquisitive, and calculative are preferred to those that are meditative, wondering, and poetic.

Here, once again, in the downgrading of subjectivity, the envy of the receptive shines forth; for given their physiology it is comparatively easier for women to develop the subjective point of view (Götz, "Masculine/Feminine," 26-30).   Subjectivity, therefore, is but another reminder to men of the receptivity they lack and have to struggle for.

WOMB PURCHASE

Men's (pre-reflective) awareness of their lack of receptivity has led them to acquire female bodies, womb-vagina systems that they can call their own, with which they can identify, or which they can assimilate to themselves, thus constituting "one flesh." Men would thus have what they lack. For it must be noted that the framers of this point of view (that man and woman in marriage will make up "one flesh") were men, not women.

Paul states that the husband is "the head of the woman" (*Ephes.* 5:23), and that he is to love her as he loves his own body, "for he who loves his wife, loves himself" (*Ephes.* 5:28). In the context of *Genesis* 2:24 ("the two will be one flesh"), the image created here is that of a "conjugal centaur, the man with a woman's body" (Stannard 314); that is, a vagina-womb system with a male *head* and a female *hole*. The image occurs earlier in Greek mythology when Zeus *swallows* Metis, thus making her one with himself. In Paul, however, the image is sanctified by being made a symbol of the union of Christ and *his* Church (*f.*), whose head he is (*Ephes.* 5:23). But this requires that Christ "rise" from the tomb, and not merely because if he didn't rise our faith in the resurrection — in our own resurrection — would be in vain. The androgyny of a "head-in-the-womb" (the aniconic *yoni-linga* sculptures of Hindu temples) is threatening to the male, who may see himself as castrated, as "in the shape of a woman." Patriarchy thrives upon the worship of an ithyphallic god, the "Risen" Christ.

In the context of earlier traditions, Chinese, Greek, and Jewish, Paul is simply presenting the Christian version of the notion that man is incomplete and needs to perfect himself through union with a woman. This incompleteness of man is often taken to mean that he cannot bear children. By marriage, however, he acquires what he lacks, the capacity to give birth. The subsequent social arrangements — the legalization of marriage; turning the husband into the juridical *head* of the wife (wives lost their family names by marriage; they could not own property, could not vote, could not have an independent career); forbidding birth-control and divorce *initiated by a woman*; and so forth — all flowed logically out of this chimerical image.

But clearly, the incompleteness of men includes also their lack of distinctive receptive systems. Possessing the system is logically prior to using it, which is logically and physiologically prior to its producing offspring. Moreover, the Pauline image does not intrinsically connote maternity, but simply the union of male and female.

It is easy to see, also, the importance of possessing a woman (a womb) for the identity of a man. Since male identity is centered around the penis, and since the vagina is correlative to the penis (vagina:penis::hole:peg), it can be seen how easy it is for men to consider the vagina as oriented or directed toward themselves, as "their" hole, a hole that desires their penis, that is waiting to be penetrated, and possessing which they are relationally fulfilled (Mairs 81).

It must be stressed that this image of oneness through possession ("the two shall be one flesh") is worlds removed from the simple coincidence of opposites that we call androgyny. In androgyny there is equality, balance, integration, not possession and subordination, as in the Pauline model. Further, when the "conjugal centaur" is understood primarily as the effort to *possess* womb-vagina systems as receptive rather than as creative, other aberrant behaviors become more clearly (though not completely) understood. According to Una Stannard (315),

> A husband when his wife died wore only a black armband because he had been deprived merely of a replaceable part, a part a man used to feel he had the right to divorce from him if it proved to be incapable of performing its function, which was why Henry VIII kept replacing one "womban" with another in his quest for a son. A husband could also separate himself from his "womban" if it was contaminated with another man's seed, wifely fornication being the unpardonable sin, but perhaps not just because it could produce children not the husband's. Perhaps when a man unconsciously regarded his wife's womb as his womb, he unconsciously reacted to her fornicating with another man as if his own body had been sexually violated, homosexually violated. A man's unconscious belief his wife's body was himself may also explain why men have often treated sexual intercourse as a form of autoeroticism and preferred women to seem like the life-size rubber dolls sold in sex shops and were genuinely puzzled by complaints of sexual dissatisfaction.

Similarly, incest becomes somewhat more clearly subsumed into this possessive strain. For the sexual violation of little girls (and boys) by their fathers or other male relatives can hardly have procreation as its purpose, but easily reflects the urge to possess womb-vagina systems — that is, complementary receptivities easier to control and less voracious than those of adult women (or men).

In a less violent way, the sexual adult, male interest in innocent prepubescent and pubescent little girls was chronicled in the paintings and sculptures of all major Western cultures, achieving some kind of frenzy during the nineteenth century with the addition of photography. Thus, according to Dijkstra,

> a genre was born in which crass child pornography disguised itself as a tribute to the ideal of innocence, and even children fell victim to man's fearful retreat from women who knew too much about the sins of the flesh. Afraid to deal with women who were strong and independent and who dared make demands, the late nineteenth century male molded the child into the image of a woman he could handle (Dijkstra 195).

Men's walking out on the first performance of Ibsen's *A Doll's House* was not so much an expression of shocked morality and outrage as of sheer fear. Conversely, Edna Pontellier's drowning in Kate Chopin's *The Awakening* conveyed the message that anything was preferable to the dainty, deprived, desultory, and self-destroying existence women were subjected to at the time.

From this point of view, prostitution itself, which is explicitly nongenerative in purpose (at least under patriarchy), may be seen as an effort to satisfy not merely a sexual urge, but the unconscious desire to possess complementary receptive systems, and to feel, at least temporarily, whole but without commitments.

HER WEAKNESS, HIS STRENGTH

During the nineteenth century the ideal was that women should live in their homes "like nuns," in the strictest sense. They were to be as pure as their husbands were not. The men sallied into the business world and thereby got their spirits sullied by the impurities of trade. The purity of the wife, therefore, was not sought *for itself*, or *for the women themselves*, but *for the men's sake*, for their prestige. This may seem a trite matter, but it will be remembered that it was the redundance of a woman's virtue upon the importance of her husband that started the Roman Republic. Lucretia's virtue won prestige for her husband and jealousy from his cousin, who raped her in revenge. Lucretia killed herself, and the news of her violation and death inspired the revolt against Tarquinius Superbus and the birth of the Republic.

The expectation that wives would live "like nuns" was taken quite literally. Sex, even within marriage, was deemed unspiritual for their men, or so the theory went. But since the species must go on, some, like Comte, proposed artificial insemination as a way to circumvent intercourse. If sex was indecorous, creativity was not.

Still, physical weakness and loss of health were considered proof that a woman was actually in pursuit of her domestic sainthood. Hence the search for, or at least acceptance of, ill health as a proof of saintliness, as in the case of Thérèse of Lisieux. Health was considered unusual, even unnatural, in a self-sacrificing woman. "To be ill," as Dijkstra remarks, "was actually thought to be a sign of delicacy and breeding" (27), and an indication of a husband's opulence.

"Death," says Dijkstra, "became a woman's ultimate sacrifice of her being to the males she had been born to serve" (29). She became, thus, a substitute Christ figure, dying for her husband in *sutti*, for her Hamlet as Ophelia, and for all men throughout the centuries.

The point here is, I think, that the "cult of invalidism," as Dijkstra calls it, in effect controlled women and placed them in a subordinate position. Again, it is impossible to avoid the message that, unless they were so controlled, women would have been there shaming men by their strength, perspicacity, business acumen, and, yes, sexuality. Starve the competition and you have won your day. And why would this have been done except that men feared women's prowess? But she must not compete with him. Rather, she was expected to transfer her powers to her husband. And even though these powers were perceived to be virtues, the powers of receptivity could not have been included. The husband became more creative the more his wife's receptivity was obliterated; he showed up stronger the fewer competing qualities his wife manifested, and the fewer the weaknesses that were detected in him.

NOTES

    1. Michael S. Kimmel, "Women-hating in Perspective," *Psychology Today*, XXI, No. 4 (April 1987), p. 71, reviewing Bram Dijkstra's overpowering book, *Idols of*

Perversity: Fantasies of Feminine Evil in Fin-de-Siècle Culture (New York: Oxford University Press, 1987). See also Dworkin, *Intercourse*, 64-65, and Wheelis 5-6.

2. It seems to me that a mature, healthy, loving, caring, and even metaphysical desire for intercourse in men may reflect the wish to penetrate "from the known into the unknown world, seeking a spiritual message of deliverance and healing" (Henderson 156); or it may be the wish to merge, to be received, to effect really the "coincidence of opposites" that mirrors or symbolizes the divine Noumenon. In a context in which such a wish is actively, freely, lovingly, and even metaphysically drawn to fruition by a woman, one cannot speak of *abuse*. In fact, even *use* would be inappropriate.

3. A. Nicholas Groth, *Men Who Rape* (New York: Plenum Press, 1979), p. 2, calls rape "a pseudosexual act." See also Sylvana Tomaselli and Roy Porter, eds., *Rape* (London: Basil Blackwell Ltd., 1986); Susan Brownmiller, *Against Our Will* (New York: Simon & Schuster, 1975).

4. *The Kreutzer Sonata*, quoted in Dworkin, *Intercourse*, p. 10. See also p. 63.

5. According to the *Genesis* account (which is, of course, patriarchal), woman "sides" with nature (tree, serpent, symbols of the Goddess) and therefore she is punished by being made to *serve* the male: she is "in labor" both when producing offspring and when producing food. But *Genesis* 1:26 and 28 was read to mean that God had placed humankind above nature, to own and subdue it. If woman was nature, then she, too, had to be subdued and dominated. And if, as happened with the advent of Christianity, nature was to be devalued *vis-à-vis* supernature, then woman, too, had to be devalued. The parallel was obvious. As God was above the earth he had created, so was man to rule over woman, so was spirit to be over matter, the soul over the body, the Church over "the world." Rosemary Radford Ruether writes: "We cannot criticize the hierarchy of male over female without ultimately criticizing and overcoming the hierarchy of humans over nature" (73). See also Sherry B. Ortner, "Is Female to Male as Nature Is to Culture?" in M. Z. Rosaldo and L. Lamphere, eds., *Woman, Culture and Society* (Stanford: Stanford University Press, 1974), pp. 67-87.

6. Eusebius, *Histor. Eccle.* IV.29. I am simplifying, of course. The myriad Gnostic variants of this theme cannot be summarized here. See, among others, Hans Jonas, *The Gnostic Religion* (Boston: Beacon Press, 1963); and Derrick Sherwin Bailey, *Sexual Relations in Christian Thought* (New York: Harper & Brothers, 1959), Chapters 1-3.

Chapter 5

More of the Same

The evidence of the self-aggrandizing of male creativity is extensive. Much remains to be researched. This chapter, therefore, continues the exploration of religious beliefs and social practices and myths in which male avoidance of receptivity and emphasis on creativity can be detected.

HEAVENLY MALES

In Christianity, mortality becomes "fundamentally unnatural" (Ruether 248) because it is a result of the Fall. It is, in other words, a punishment, though in the long run the Fall becomes the *Felix culpa* that deserved redemption by Christ.[1]

If death is introduced by the Fall, was there need of reproduction before it? And if not, was there need of sexual dimorphism? St. Thomas Aquinas (*STh* 1, 99, 2) even wonders if there would have been need of women before the Fall (the need of men is not questioned), but concludes that there would have been, for difference in sex is "natural." However, he says, God would have created this natural difference because of his foreknowledge of the Fall. Before the Fall, coitus would have taken place without concupiscence, and this is the state that will be reinstated in the resurrection: "they will be like the angels of God" (*erunt sicut angeli Dei*)(*Mt* 22:30).

Theoretically at least, angels are sexless beings, but in fact, in the Hebrew (*elohim*), the Christian (*angelloi; angeli*), and the Muslim traditions (*malâ'ikah; Qu'rân*, Sûrah 53:26), they are male. The angelic/virginal, sexless state, is male *par excellence*. It can be understood how so much Patristic thought implies, or states explicitly, that virginity is a male characteristic, and that for a woman, to become a virgin (both here and hereafter) is to become a male!

The theology here is logical. If Christ, being *immortal*, assumed *mortal* human nature (*Philip.* 2:5-11), in the resurrection we, *mortals*, shall assume *immortal*, divine-like nature. The logic continues: we will be immortal because we will be likened to Christ, who is male: "Predestined to be conformed to the image of his Son" (*Rom.* 8:29).

A problem is thus posed: if femaleness is "natural," yet in heaven all will be "male" (*sicut angeli*), what happens to women in heaven? The answer comes in *The Gospel of Thomas*. Simon Peter suggests that Mary should leave them, "for women are not worthy of Life [in the Kingdom of Heaven]." Jesus replies: "'I myself shall lead her in order to make her male, so that she too may become a living spirit resembling you males. For every woman who will make herself male will enter the Kingdom of Heaven'" (*logion* 114; Robinson 130).

How will this come to pass? Even though women will rise *as women* (for that is nature, says Augustine), their femaleness shall be changed: "The female members shall remain adapted not to the old uses, but to a new beauty, which, so far from provoking lust, now extinct, shall excite praise to the wisdom and clemency of God" (*De Civ. Dei*, XII.17). In the resurrection, even women shall be heavenly males!

The sense that it is the female organs that are sexual, alluring, and tempting (that is, threatening) is impossible to escape. Women will be allowed in heaven only as half-males, as desexed, neutered, and rendered harmless to the fearful males.

But there is more. The requirements of heavenly masculinization have been pushed here on earth, but not consistently. For example, the statement in the *Vatican Declaration* of 1976 that "there must be a physical resemblance between the priest and Christ" (Section 27) implies that, in the words of Rosemary Ruether, "the possession of male genitalia becomes essential prerequisite for representing Christ" (126). While this is consonant with the view of the "heavenly male," it is contrary to the ages-long advocacy of the imitation of Christ by men and women, brothers, priests, and nuns.

Genesis 1:27 proclaims the creation of man and woman "in God's image," and Paul, unawares of the use his words would be put to in the future, insists again and again that in Christ there is neither male nor female (*Gal.* 3:20), and that therefore it is appropriate, nay, required of Christians to imitate Christ in the same way as all human beings "imitate" Adam (that is, possess Adam's nature): "Just as we have borne the image of the terrestrial [Adam], let us also bear the image of the Celestial [Christ]" (*1 Cor.* 15:49). In fact, Paul saw the Christian's life as a progressive changing into the likeness of Christ (*2 Cor.* 3:18) — not of an abstract or amorphous Christ, but clearly of the risen Christ, glorious humanity and all (Crouzel 62).

Commenting on these and similar passages (e.g., *Rom.* 6:5; *Philip.* 2:5 ff. and 3:10), Henri Crouzel writes:

> By the help of words whose roots are *homoios* and *morphê*, Paul expresses a change of resemblance between the incarnate Christ, who has taken on the human condition, and the people he directs toward his divine condition. He has taken up the form (*morphê*) of servant, making himself similar (*en homoiômati*) to people. We must, in turn, through baptism, become "grafted onto him" (*symphytoi*) in resemblance (*tô homoiômati*) of his death so as to obtain the resemblance of his resurrection (Crouzel 61).

It is obvious that if this *homoiosis* is to be real and meaningful *for women*, either Christ must be deemed androgynous or, what comes to the same thing, his maleness must be judged irrelevant. That was probably Paul's mind, at least to judge from his words. But soon after, the imitation of Christ was interpreted as involving masculinization. The apocryphal *Gospel of Thomas* (*logion* 114, cited above) maintains that for a woman to become "like" Christ, she must become "like a man," and Augustine, as was pointed above, adopted this view *vis-à-vis* the heavenly reality of women.

The fact must be stressed that the imitation of Christ that has been expected of all Christians, male and female, has not been — has *never* been — a matter only of imagination and prayer. In many instances it entailed martyrdom, for women as well as for men. But if women were considered *imitatores Christi* in their deaths, it hardly seems reasonable to assert that they cannot imitate Christ as priests because they are not male. If the maleness of Christ was no obstacle to the *imitatio Christi* in martyrdom, and if it will be no obstacle to women's masculinization in heaven, how can it be so for the imitation of Christ in the priesthood? Obviously, what we have here is not a good theological argument but the *semblance* of one.

I am not saying that the theology of masculinization is acceptable in any way. What I am pointing out is that ordinary logic does not allow one to draw *only* the conclusions one prefers. If the *imitatio Christi* requires masculinization both here and hereafter, then Christ's maleness is no obstacle. How can it, then, be called an obstacle to women's ordination to the priesthood?

And what is the theology of masculinization but a high-sounding attempt to convert women into men, to deny their receptivity, and to make male creativity triumphant even in heaven?

WHOSE BODY?

Over millennia, women have been the prime feeders of humanity. In hunting-gathering societies they were the primary gatherers. Hunting was precarious, even at the best of times, so the gatherers were the regular providers. Once agriculture took root, women shared in the tasks of sowing and reaping, thus continuing their feeding roles.

As providers of food, women have labored at all kinds of tasks. Just a cursory look at any collection of mediaeval and renaissance paintings and illuminations will reveal the diversity of jobs women performed. All of them were in some measure related to the feeding of their families.

But more fundamentally, women feed children out of their own bodies. Our first food is our mothers' milk, and that food is produced in and delivered through their bodies. In a true sense, a lactating woman could whisper to her infant, "Suck, drink: this is my body!" In the long process of patriarchalization such an important — nay, essential — role could not have been left un-masculinized. Moses, with the power of YHWH, "rained" manna from heaven (*Ex.* 16:12-33; *John* 6:31-32). Jesus fed the multitude (*Mt.* 14:17-21), and in a final metaphor, offered his body for bread and his blood for wine to his followers (*John* 6:35; *Mt.* 26:26-29), instituting a commemorative rite. Shortly after, Ignatius of Antioch († *ca.* 110) labeled himself "wheat of God, to be ground by the molars of wild beasts and turned into white bread" (*Ad Rom.* 4).

As the Christian hierarchy grew in power, the feeding role that was naturally woman's became appropriated by the male priests. The celebration of the eucharist became more a banquet than a sacrifice, and communion acquired importance. In fact, the practice for many centuries was, and in some Christian denominations still is, to receive communion before any other food, solid or liquid, is taken. A "natural fast" (*ieiunium naturale*) is to be observed from midnight till communion time (*Codex Iuris Canonici* [1917], No. 858.1). Explaining this ancient practice, Isidore of Seville wrote: "Thus it pleased the Holy Spirit to ordain through the Apostles that to honor it, the sacrament of the Lord's Body should enter the Christian's mouth before any other food; and therefore throughout the entire world this custom is kept" (*De Offic. Eccle.*, I.18.3 [ML 83, 754 *ff.*]).

Only priests are permitted to administer this food, handle it, distribute it. Tertullian writes, "We receive the sacrament of the Eucharist . . . only from the hands of him who presides" (*De Coron.*, III.3), and the Council of Trent, in its twenty-second Session, Chapter 1, declared that Jesus had created the priesthood to perpetuate the Eucharist.

God, male YHWH, was compared to a mother feeding her children; Moses's manna was seen as prefigurement of the eucharist; and in general all natural food became a symbol of spiritual nourishment. In his catechesis, Cyril of Jerusalem explained it thus: "This is the grace of which Solomon spoke in *Ecclesiastes*: 'Come,' he says, 'eat your bread' (your spiritual bread, that is), 'with joy'" (*Cat. Mystag.* IV [= XXII]; MG 33, 1104). John Damascene also writes: "Bread and wine are used because God knows human weakness very well, how we reject what is not familiar to us . . . . Therefore, as people usually eat bread and drink water and wine, he united to these his divinity, and made them his body and blood, so that through ordinary and natural things we might obtain what is beyond nature" (*De Fide Ortho.*, IV.3; MG 94, 1136 *ff.*).

As spirit (*m.*) became more important than flesh (*f.*), spiritual food grew in importance over natural, material food, and the providers of spiritual food (men, priests) replaced the dispensers of ordinary food (mothers, women).

WOMEN PRIESTS

Once masculinized, great efforts were made to retain the control of spiritual food — indeed, of all spiritual matters. Hence the systematic exclusion of women from the (male) priesthood.

The evidence for labeling sexist this exclusion of women from the male domain of the priesthood is readily at hand. Anglicans and Episcopalians (with decreasing success), Roman Catholics, and the Orthodox Churches, have explicitly argued that priests should be men because Jesus was a man. The most cogent theological reasoning against the ordination of women is called the "fittingness" argument. I want to show through a *reductio ad absurdum* that if the argument holds, the cardinal Christian belief in Jesus's salvific death would lose its truth (Dinter, differently).

Briefly, the "argument from fittingness" states that the sacraments the priest administers, especially the eucharist, are symbolic acts, and that their symbolic power is based on the *natural* character of the connection between the symbol and the symbolized — for example, cleansing water and (cleansing) baptism. Since Jesus, whose saving acts the sacraments symbolize, was a man, the priest must himself be a man. Without this maleness there would be no "natural resemblance" between symbol and symbolized.

Before tackling the argument, three general comments seem appropriate. First, Jesus was not *only* male: he was a male *Jew*. Jewishness was as distinctive as maleness. If the "argument from fittingness" held truly, then all persons acting *in persona Christi* would have to be *both* male *and* Jewish. Maleness is no more (nor less) distinguishable *from the reality of the historical Jesus* than is his Jewishness. The fact that only maleness is singled out as significant in the "fittingness argument" is clear evidence of sexist prejudice in the same way as Christian anti-Semitism was a sign of prejudice, since it overlooked the historical fact of Jesus's Jewishness when it persecuted the Jews.

Second, femaleness has not been, in the past, an obstacle to the recognition of Jesus in the person of his ministers. Women have been symbols of Christ, as in the case of many female saints. Specifically, there is the case of Blandina, one of the Martyrs of Lyons (*ca.* 177), who "through her ardent prayers stimulated great enthusiasm in those undergoing their ordeal, who in their agony saw with their outward eyes in the person of their sister the One who was crucified for them" (Eusebius, *Hist. Eccl.*, V.1.41)

Thirdly, maleness is essential to Jesus only historically or *ex post facto* — that is, from the fact that what was cannot not have been, and that since there was a person called Jesus who was male and a Jew, Jesus's maleness and Jewishness remain historically necessary. But aside from this historical necessity maleness is not essential to Jesus. And it won't do to say that maleness is essential to Jesus because he was the Son of God — that is, the Second (male) Person of the Trinity. For theologically, even if we admit that God is male and Father, there is no inherent reason why the Second Person could not have been female, a daughter, incarnate as a woman (as Mother Ann Lee, "Mother Ann the Christ," claimed to be in the eighteenth century). Filiation does not intrinsically necessitate sonhood. Filiation is merely the relation that properly makes anyone a son or daughter; in the Trinity, it is the relation that constitutes the Second Person, which would be thus constituted even if it were a daughter. The only theological reason for sonhood is Jesus's own statement that *he* was the Son, a statement which is open to a multitude of interpretations.

More specifically, however, the "argument from fittingness" is theologically aberrant because of what it denies implicitly. Curiously, its proponents do not seem to realize that what appears as a strength in the argument — the naturalness of the symbol — is a scorpion sting. If the argument held, it would undermine the belief in the universality of the salvific act of Christ. For in maintaining that the maleness of the priest is necessary for a natural resemblance of symbol to symbolized, the argument implicitly restricts human nature to maleness by claiming that the maleness of Jesus is what must be symbolized, implying thereby that maleness was the essence of the *human nature* assumed in him. If that were the case, only males would have been redeemed by Christ.

Original sin is believed to affect human nature regardless of gender, time, place, and so on. The sin of Adam and Eve affects human nature; not male nature and female nature separately, but *human* nature, which is understood to include both men and women. Christ's saving action is supposed to effect a radical change in human nature involving both men and women. And here, the fact that Jesus was historically male *cannot* be invoked in any way, for it would entail the denial of the universality of the salvific act. If the man Jesus died for all, men and women, Jews and Gentiles, then the maleness of Jesus was not significant for salvation; if that is so, then it cannot be brought in surreptitiously as an argument for the ordination of men only — not any more logically than one could maintain that men are more "fittingly" saved by the man Jesus, or that men symbolize redemption more "fittingly"; or that the *imitatio Christi* is more "fittingly" performed by men. I shall now elaborate these notions in detail.

The sin of Adam and Eve affected human *nature*. To be effective, redemption had to affect human *nature*, too. Theologically, Christ's incarnation implies union between the divine person-*nature* of the Word and a human nature (body-soul), forming a being possessing one divine personhood and two natures, divine and human. The human nature thus united to the divine was human nature *simpliciter*, that is, regardless of gender, time, place, and so on. This understanding of the term *nature* implies that human nature is essentially the same regardless of specifications of gender, time, color, and so on. If this were not so, the ancients would not have been human, nor would patagonians, nor slaves (as was maintained). Theologically, if this were not so, women would not have been redeemed, nor would any other men except those Jews, sons of carpenters, living in Palestine during the first decades of the Common Era. The universality of Christ's redemptive act hinges on the fact that it is human *nature per se* that is united hypostatically (that is, in only one person) to the divine nature in the divine Person of the Word. Because it is human *nature* that is so united, Christ's actions have a collective or universal significance and influence upon all individuals possessing that nature, regardless of gender, color, nationality, and so on.

This has been the understanding of Scripture, of the Fathers, and of the theologians. *John* 1:14 states that the Word became flesh (*ho logos sarx egenneto*). The Latin translation keeps the meaning: *Verbum caro factum est*. The early credal formulas translate *caro* into *homo*: *homo factus est*, but the meaning of *homo* is not gender-specific; rather, it retains the meaning of *caro*. The fact that *homo* is used to mean *human nature* implies an incipient theologizing.

The theologizing develops. St. Ignatius of Antioch calls Christ "that unique physician, both carnal and spiritual, born and unborn, God existing in flesh" (*Ad Ephes.* 7). Tertullian calls Christ "man meshed with God [*homo Deo mixtus*]" (*Apologet.*, XXI.4). The Word, he says, put on flesh, but did not change into flesh, for that would have entailed the cessation of divinity. The scriptural expression, "become flesh" (*caro factus*), he equates to "putting on flesh" (*indutus*) (*Adversus Prax.* 27:6-15). This entails that "the property of each substance [= nature] is preserved" (*salva est utriusque proprietas substantiae*) (*Adversus Prax.* 27 line 64). The theologizing continues:

> It is not fit that the Son of God should be born of a human father's seed, lest, if he were wholly the son of a man, he should fail to be also the Son of God. . . . In order, therefore, that he who was already the Son of God . . . might also be the son of man, he only wanted to assume flesh, human flesh, without human seed. . . . He is thus man-with-God — that is, human flesh with God's divinity. . . . Christ possesses both substances [= natures], that of the flesh and that of the divinity (*De Carne Christi*, XVII, 1-3, 6-7).

Tertullian's words become a formula repeated through the centuries. Leo the Great uses it and clarifies it by adding the term "nature": "Maintaining, therefore, the properties of each nature and substance [*salva igitur proprietate utriusque naturae et substantiae*]" (*Letter to Flavian* 3). And again: "Preserving, therefore, the substance of both natures, and uniting them in one Person, lowliness is assumed by Majesty, infirmity by Power, mortality by Immortality . . . as was needed for our healing" (*De Myst. Nativit.*, 2; ML 54, 190).

Because nature is understood both as concrete and as communicable, the assumption of human nature in Christ entails the healing of human nature *in all humans*. St. Paul states this clearly: "Sending his own Son in the likeness of sinful flesh, and for sin, he condemned sin in the flesh" (*Rom.* 8:3). St. Irenæus continued this trend of thought: "It was necessary that he who began to destroy sin and redeem humans worthy of death, should be like those redeemed — that is, human, so that sin should be destroyed by a human, thus freeing humans from death. . . . What he seemed to be [i.e., human], he was: God taking up the old form that he should slay sin and revive humanity (*Adv. Haeres.*, III, 18, 7). St. Ambrose also states: "He took from us what he should offer for us as his own, to redeem us from ourselves. . . . For what was the reason of the incarnation except that the flesh that had sinned should be redeemed by the flesh?" (ML 16, 832). St. Leo also makes it abundantly clear that the consequence of this union of natures is the regeneration of humanity: "Being then born truly man, our Lord Jesus Christ, who never ceases to be true God, made himself the beginning of a new creature, and in the manner of his birth has given man a spiritual foundation . . . since the descent of God to what was human has brought about the raising of man to what is divine" (*Ad Nativit. Sermo*, VII, 2; ML 54, 216). And St. Ephræm: "He is born from God according to his nature and from man beyond his nature . . . that we may be born from man according to our nature and from God beyond our nature" (*Sermo de Domino Nostro*, I, 150). St. Thomas Aquinas summarizes the theologizing: "This word man [he writes] signifies human nature according as it is made to be in a suppositum [i.e., as it exists in each person]. . . . And hence it cannot properly be said that the Son assumed a man, since . . . in Christ there is but one suppositum and one hypostasis [= person]" (*STh* 3, 4, 3). Again he writes: "The word man signifies human nature in the concrete, according as it is in the suppositum; and hence, since we cannot say a suppositum was assumed, so we cannot say a man was assumed" (*STh* 3, 2, 3 *ad* 2).

This does not mean that human nature, as assumed, is to be understood merely as a universal concept, a generalization from the real lives of human beings. If this were the case, the assumption of human nature by the divinity would be purely fictional, with no concrete consequences for salvation; and Jesus's body would be illusory, as was maintained by the Docetists. No. Nature is that concrete something in an individual which is concretely present in all other individuals of the same class.

Nature *by itself*, apart from individuals, does not exist; it is a mere concept. Nature exists as individuals having that nature exist concretely. Nature is known only intellectually; but this does not mean it exists only intellectually.

When we speak of human nature we mean those concrete traits or characteristics that are concretely present whenever a human being concretely and individually exists. Without concretely and individually existing, human nature does not exist — except as a concept. When the nature that exists concretely and individually is a "rational" nature, we call the compact "person." That is the definition of person originated by Boëthius: person is an individual having concretely, existentially, a "rational" or "intellectual" nature (*Individuum subsistens in natura intellectuali*) (*De Duabus Natur.* Chapter 3; ML 64, 3143). St. Thomas maintains (*STh* 3, 4, 4 *ad* 3) that human nature was *not* assumed as (or in) an already fully constituted, concretely living human person. The Word did not assume a born man. Human nature was assumed as it would have existed concretely in an individual. The individual thus formed was Jesus.

The concretion of human nature with the individuating characteristics of body and soul, which normally constitutes for us the born individual human being, was anomalous both in that the *person* thus constituted had a personhood preexisting as the Word, and in that by virtue of that personhood it already had a nature, the divine nature. Hence the Incarnation was a union of concrete natures in a preexisting Person, the Word. The concretion of all this was the God-Man Jesus.

The conclusion is obvious: the fact that Jesus was historically male has absolutely no significance for salvation. Human nature could just as easily have been assumed in the concrete as a woman. Since theologically there is no repugnance in claiming that the Second Person could have been a Daughter, there is no theological objection to that Daughter becoming incarnate as a woman, Christa. From a soteriological point of view, there would have been no difference. Therefore, it does not seem reasonable to accept this in the theology of the incarnation and redemption, and to deny it in the theology of the sacraments — especially the priesthood. The argument from "fittingness" is thus but a vain rationalization for excluding women from a male domain. In other words, it is plain and unadulterated sexist double-talk.

IMMORTALITY

In a crucial theological passage, St. Paul writes:

Now if this is what we proclaim, that Christ was raised from the dead, how can some of you say there is no resurrection from the dead? If there be no resurrection, then Christ was not raised; and if Christ was not raised, then our gospel is null and void, and so is your faith; and we turn out to be lying witnesses for God, because we bore witness that he raised Christ to life, whereas, if the dead are not raised, he did not raise him. For if the dead are not raised, it follows that Christ was not raised; and if Christ was not raised, your faith has nothing in it and you are still in your old state of sin. It follows also that those who have died in Christ's fellowship are utterly lost. If it is only for this life that Christ has given us hope, we of all men are most to be pitied (*1 Cor.* 15:12-19).

According to Paul, the resurrection of Christ is the central, nay pivotal belief of Christianity. Without it, the belief that the Christian will be raised cannot be maintained, because the resurrection is the "proof" that God, in Christ, has destroyed the power of sin — certainly the effect of sin, which is death. Sin — the sin of Adam and Eve (the Fall) — ushered in death, for death would not have existed in Eden: Adam and Eve (and their descendants) would not have died. Christ died to restore Eden; that is, to eliminate sin's consequence, death. Resurrection, then, which entails the overcoming of death as final and the reintroduction of immortality, is the proof that this "buying back" (re-[d]-emption) of Eden has taken place.

My task here is not a critique of the theology of resurrection and the belief in eternal life. Rather, I wish to show that faith in — nay, concern with — resurrection, even though spread far beyond the reaches of Christianity and present in many pre-Christian traditions, is primarily a male idea, and that its imposition upon all the faithful is but another manifestation of patriarchal sexism.

Stated very generally, belief in an after-life is found in many of the earth's religions. In fact, such a belief (and certain practices associated with it, such as burial) appear in very ancient, prehistorical times. Beliefs in a transcendent realm are present in China, India, Iran, Egypt, Greece, Sumer, among the Norsemen, as well as in tribal faiths. Myths of death and resurrection, such as those of Isis and Osiris, Sisyphus, Inanna, Jesus, and others, appear with such frequency as to constitute a pattern. In Judaism, at the beginning, enduring is collective rather than individual, until the Exile. Then individual concerns start, and the resurrection of the body is introduced. At first, this is to take place in some kind of millennium (*Is.* 65:17-23), one of whose major purposes is to redress injustice. The pattern is similar to that of Greek belief as depicted by Plato (*Republic*, X.608-620; *Phaedo* 69E-115A; *Phaedrus* 245C-249D); as yet "no immortality but a blessed longevity is the ideal" (Ruether 239). Eventually, under Greek and, later, Christian influence, belief in individual resurrection of the body begins, culminating in the statements of Maimonides's "Thirteen Principles" and his Essay on Resurrection.

Neither in Judaism nor in Egyptian religion is there a strict dogma about the resurrection. Job's

> I know my vindicator lives,
> A guarantor upon the dust will stand;
> Even after my skin is flayed,
> In my crumbling flesh I shall see God (*Job* 19:25-26)

must be countered by the Qôhéleth's "I commend enjoyment, for we have no other good in this life than to eat and drink and be happy. This will accompany us in our struggle during the few years which God grants us beneath the sun" (*Ecclesiastes* 8:15).

In Egypt, the "Harpers' Songs" proclaim the value of this life over the next, as is clear from this sample:

> (vi,2)
> Follow your heart and your happiness,
> do your things on earth as your heart commands!
> When there comes to you that day of mourning,
> the Weary-hearted hears not their mourning;
> wailing saves no man from the pit.
>
> (vii,2)
> Refrain:
> Make holiday,
> Do not weary of it!
> Lo, none is allowed to take his goods with him,
> Lo, none who departs comes back again! (Lichtheim, I, 196-197).

And when the famous "man" in *Papyrus 3024* of the Berlin Museum contemplates suicide, his soul (his *ba*) tells him, "Enjoy life *here*! Forget about the beyond" (Reed 79; Thomas 166).

But this does not mean that desire and, even, the quest for immortality was not a part of the scene, especially (almost uniquely) for men. The best example is, perhaps, Gilgamesh. Right from the beginning, Gilgamesh is warned that immortality is not to be his lot. A dream he has is interpreted for him by his friend Enkidu: "The meaning of the dream is this. The father of the gods [Enlil] has given you kingship, such is your destiny, everlasting life is not your destiny" (Sandars 70). The interpretation holds no particular threat to Gilgamesh at the time. He is full of vigor and desirous of adventure. But after the affair with the "Bull of Heaven," Enkidu is stricken and dies. Gilgamesh mourns him, aware, too, that Enkidu's fate will one day belong to him: "How can I rest, how can I be at peace? Despair is in my heart. What my brother is now, that shall I be when I am dead. Because I am afraid of death I will go as best as I can to find Utnapishtim whom they call the Faraway, for he has entered the assembly of the gods [he has become immortal]" (Sandars 97). To Siduri, the woman who asks him about his quest and the state of his health, he answers: "Because of my brother [Enkidu] I am afraid of death, because of my brother I stray through the wilderness and cannot rest. But now, young woman, maker of wine, since I have seen your face do not let me see the face of death which I dread so much" (Sandars 101-102). To Urshanabi he says: "I am afraid of death, therefore, Urshanabi, tell me which is the road to Utnapishtim? If it is possible I will cross the waters of death; if not I will wander still farther through the wilderness" (Sandars 104). Finally, Gilgamesh stands in front of Utnapishtim and begs him: "How shall I find the life for which I am searching?" (Sandars 106). Utnapishtim's answer is clear and unambiguous: "There is no permanence. Do we build a house to stand for ever, do we seal a contract to hold for all time? Do brothers divide an inheritance to keep for ever, does the flood-time of the rivers endure?" (Sandars 106-107). Utnapishtim's answer echoes Enlil's dream and Siduri's words: "Gilgamesh, where are you hurrying to? You will never find that life for which you are looking. When the gods created man they allotted to him death, but life they retained in their own keeping" (Sandars 102).

But Gilgamesh is deaf to her and to Utnapishtim's words, just as he had been to Enkidu's explanation. Down, under water, he plunges, where he spies a special plant growing, whose name he calls, "The Old Men are Young Again" (Sandars 116). If immortality is unattainable, at least perpetual youth will be his, and he will take back that boon to his subjects in Uruk. But that was not to be. When he was within sight of Uruk, he

> saw a well of cool water and he went down and bathed; but deep in the pool there was lying a serpent, and the serpent sensed the sweetness of the flower. It rose out of the water and snatched it away, and immediately it sloughed its skin and returned to the well. Then Gilgamesh sat down and wept, and tears ran down his face (Sandars 117).

The story concludes with a retelling of the words of Enlil, the words Enkidu had interpreted for Gilgamesh: "You were given the kingship, such was your destiny, everlasting life was not your destiny" (Sandars 118).

Centuries later Miguel de Unamuno notes that hunger for immortality is the focal point of religion. It is, also, denied by death. That is the paradox of existence, the "tragic sense of life." He writes:

> I must confess, painful though the confession be, that in the days of the simple faith of my childhood, descriptions of the tortures of hell, however terrible, never made me tremble, for I always felt that nothingness was much more terrifying. He who suffers lives, and he who lives suffering, even though over the portal of his abode is written "Abandon all hope!" loves and hopes (Unamuno, *Tragic*, 43).

And in an impassioned passage he cries:

> I do not want to die — no; I neither want to die nor do I want to want to die; I want to live for ever and ever and ever. I want this "I" to live — this poor "I" that I am and that I feel myself to be here and now, and therefore the problem of the duration of my soul, of my own soul, tortures me.
>
> I am the centre of my universe, the centre of the universe, and in my supreme anguish I cry with Michelet, "Mon moi, ils m'arrachent mon moi!"[2] (Unamuno, *Tragic*, 45).

Death is a fact of life; at any rate, death is a fact, even if not *of* life. But Unamuno refuses to surrender to it the longing of his self for a life that knows no end. The *fact* remains, so heaven is invented as a home port of the soul from which it will never be cast out.

In similar though less picturesque terms, Adam and Eve are expelled from Paradise. A snake has deprived them of their immortality, and lest they might find the Tree of Life, eat its fruit, and become immortal again, an angel and a flaming sword are placed at the entrance of the Garden of Eden (*Gen.* 3:22-24). But to the Gnostics, the quest for immortality is a temptation, and the expulsion from Eden, a vengeful act of a malicious Demiurge.

The Sophia Prunikos realizes she must begin to counteract the activity of her apostate son, Ialdabaoth. So she sends the serpent, her symbol, to tempt Adam and Eve with the promise of a special knowledge (*gnosis*) if they will break the command of Ialdabaoth. When they do, "their eyes are open," and for the first time the principalities of the world begin to taste defeat (Jonas 93; *Apocryphon of John* 22:10-35, in Robinson 111). Referring to the Biblical God YHWH/ Elohim, the *Testimony of Truth* asks:

> Of what sort is this God? First [he] envied Adam that he should eat from the tree of knowledge. And secondly he said, "Adam, where are you?" And God does not have foreknowledge, that is, since he did not know this from the beginning. [And] afterwards he said, "Let us cast him [out] of this place, lest he eat of the tree of life and live for ever." Surely he has shown himself to be a malicious envier. And what kind of God is this? For great is the blindness of those who read, and they did not know it (*Testimony* 47:15-48:4, in Robinson 412).

For the Gnostics, YHWH/Elohim, the God of the world, is vitally interested in preventing Adam and Eve from gaining true knowledge (*gnosis*). Part of this knowledge is that the "tree of life" is counterfeit (*Apocryphon of John* 55:18-56:17, in Jonas 92), which in Gnostic terminology means its life is not truly spiritual (*pneumatike*). From this point of view, the quest for immortality is a worldly temptation, and should not be followed.

From another point of view, however, the *Genesis* account bears witness to the struggle between the newer male God, YHWH/Elohim, and the ancient Goddess. The story lets us witness the patriarchal effort to put down the Goddess (Eve) and the symbols of her cyclical self-renewal: serpent and tree. The expulsion of Adam and Eve from Paradise is symbolic of the refusal of the life perennially renewed in woman and her symbols, in favor of the abstract, transcendent life (heaven) that may culminate a linear pilgrimage on earth. It will take centuries, but first in Judaism, and then in Christianity (and later in Islam), resurrection and life everlasting will be the male substitutes for the feminine cycle of death and rebirth.

Unamuno sees the cult of death as the desire for immortality (*Tragic* 41), and he is right in a general sense. Prehistoric burial attests to some sense of hope for a return to life. But the term "immortality" has become tinged with a peculiar linear sense different from the cyclical one it probably had originally. For Judaism after the Exile, and for Christianity after the death of Jesus, immortality has been tied up to resurrection, and resurrection has been seen as a unique event in the course of history; in fact, as the event that will mark the end of history. The resurrection will inaugurate an everlasting life, a life which will see no death, a life, therefore, which will not have cycles.

The ancient experience, however, was different. The primordial, prehistoric experience of immortality must have been cyclical, for that was the only experience of lastingness available to humans. It had to do with the cycles of the woman's body; not merely the menstrual cycles, but the cycles of the womb's engorgement and its emptying in the appearance of new human life, repeated again and again during a woman's fertile span. It had to do with the cycle of the trees, shedding their leaves and donning them again, and producing fruit in seasonal cycles. It had to do with the cycle of the grain, gathered in the summer, kept underground in silos and earthen jars; taken out for planting in the fields where it would lay dormant under the earth in order to sprout gloriously in the late spring. It had to do with the cycle of the seasons. It had to with the cycle of the snake, renewing itself by sloughing its skin — that is, being born again with every change.

The cyclical sense of immortality was kept alive in the primitive fertility rites; then in the hierogamic rituals of ancient Goddesses, such as the marriage of Inanna and Dumuzi in late summer, reenacted every year by the King and the High Priestess of the Goddess; in the myths of descent and ascent, such as those of Inanna and Persephone; and finally, in the mysteries, especially the mysteries of Dionysus and Demeter.

Death holds a lesser (or perhaps merely a different) fear for women who have experienced in their bodies the eternal though cyclical renewal of life. Thus Inanna is apprehensive about her meeting with her sister, Ereshkigal, in the dreaded underworld.   She makes arrangements just in case her stay be prolonged. But she knows that, even if she dies (which she does), she will be raised again by the gods. Interestingly, Dumuzi, her male consort, sees her death as final. He has no sense of renewal. Once she has gone, he quickly forgets about her and takes over the kingdom, earning thus her anger and contempt upon her return. Similarly, the original myth of Persephone has her deciding to spend part of the year in the underworld with those forms of life which are awaiting their return to earthly life. Her sojourn underground is her choice. But later, when the myth is masculinized, Hades kidnaps her, rapes her, and drags her underground *forever*, and only relents and accepts a compromise when Demeter refuses to sprout life again, appeals to Zeus, and the cycle is installed.

Women understand the cycle, men do not. It is the man's feminine *ba* (his soul) in Egyptian *Papyrus 3024* that counsels him to seek life *here*. It is the woman Siduri who tells Gilgamesh he will never find the kind of immortality he is looking for. Instead, she counsels the king, "fill your belly with good things; day and night, night and day, dance and be merry, feast and rejoice. Let your clothes be fresh, bathe yourself in water, *cherish the little child that holds your hand*, and make your wife happy in your embrace; for this too is the lot of man" (Sandars 102; emphasis mine). And, interestingly, when Gilgamesh is returning to Uruk with the plant "The Old Men Are Young Again," it is a self-renewing, cyclical snake that eats it, in a way, symbolically, reaffirming the understanding of immortality as renewal rather than indefinite continuance.

Calypso, it is true, promises Ulysses immortal life if he will stay with her (*Odyssey* VII.257-258); but what she really wants (and what she really offers) is a continual relationship with Ulysses. Ulysses understands the offer for what it is, not a promise of *eternal life* but of a protracted tryst. And he refuses; for, frankly, he prefers Penelope and the comforts of his own bed.

Immortality, then, seems to be primarily a concern of men (Paglia 10). The ancient texts of the Goddess, and the ancient rituals, seem to be centered around cyclical renewal. But with the rise of the newer male gods, and with the eradication of Goddess worship, the search for immortality becomes paramount. Interestingly, when Jesus brings up this notion of death and rebirth in his talk with Nicodemus, the man fails to catch his meaning, drawing this rebuke from Jesus: "Are you a teacher in Israel and you do not understand this?" (*Jo.* 3:10).

Men, it would seem, had difficulty with a return to the earth from which they came, an earth which, after all, was/is feminine, and whose womb was thus refilled. Burial in a cavernous earth was not unlike burial in a fleshly vulva, and like the latter, it raised prospects of castration and, above all, impotence. Immortality held the promise of a perpetual erection.

Christianity, above all, defined itself as a male religion right away. I do not mean by this the establishment of a male hierarchy and the exclusion of women from it, a move chronicled in the Gospels and the Apocrypha. No; I mean that Christianity was unable to live with the fact of an open cavern, an empty tomb. It could not live with the yawning nothingness of the receptive feminine; it had to fill in the vacuum, and it did so with the doctrine of the Resurrection of Christ — essentially, devotion to a Risen Head.

The question is not whether or not death is a universal phenomenon, affecting men and women equally. Of course it is. Rather, the question, asks Ruether, "is whether women have the same stake in denying their mortality through doctrines of life after death, or whether this is not the apogee of male individualism and egoism" (235).

The conclusion, I think, is inescapable. The belief in the resurrection is primarily male-centered. It is essential only to a male-centered religion. But this belief has been imposed on women, too, even against their experience and need. It is, therefore, one more example of male inability to deal with receptivity, and of the effort to compensate for it with an egoistic emphasis on creativity.

IN MEN'S IMAGE

If even for a moment we entertain the equation of masculinity with creativity and receptivity with femininity, it becomes instantly apparent how the past five thousand years of patriarchal dominance have witnessed a preeminence of the male/creative and a suppression, or at least a downgrading, of the female/receptive. Swords, daggers, rifles, canons, airplanes, autos, skyscrapers, rockets, pens; conquests, discoveries; institutions of various forms; all the multifaceted productions of the analytic intellect — what Hermann Hesse called "the father side of life" (Hesse, *Narcissus* 170) — stand up like so many phallic tributes to male creativity, whereas brothels, harems, nunneries; mothers, maids, mystics, sibyls, and secretaries (all guardians of inner sancta) make up the lowly realm of the female/receptive. It is impossible to block the realization that the achievements of civilization have been male/creative, and that energy has been spent in downgrading the feminine dimension of human existence, wonder, contemplation, receptivity. We praise strength, confidence, activity, harshness, intellection, protectiveness, adver·ᵘresomeness, and solidarity, and despise weakness, hesitation, passivity, so...ess, feelings, security, and solitude; and when we cannot get rid of these by sheer emphasis on their opposites, we trample them down in rape, chain them in prostitution, ridicule them in pornography, padlock them through marriage and abortion laws. Then, when the slaves revolt and seek equality, we impose on them that ultimate condition: success depends on their becoming "like men" — that is, on their giving up their distinctive receptive/feminine qualities and competing like creative men in a world of creators.

Thus the sum of what we term sexism becomes subsumed in the vision of a creativity desperately at odds with receptivity. Why would it be so important to create except to forestall, in some fashion, the self-damaging question of receptivity?

NOTES

1. The idea of the *Felix culpa* ("Lucky sin" or "Happy fault") is expressed clearly and poetically in the Preface at the end of the "*Exultet*" sung during the Easter Vigil: "It would have profited us nothing to have been born, unless redemption had also been given to us! O wonderful condescension of your mercy toward us! O inestimable love: to redeem a slave you delivered up your Son! O truly necessary sin of Adam which was blotted out by the death of Christ! O happy fault that merited so great a Redeemer!" (*Liber Usualis*, p. 776N).

2. "My self, they are tearing my self from me!"

Chapter 6

The Psychological Why of Sexism

In previous chapters I established the connection between creativity and masculinity, and between receptivity and femininity. I showed, also, by reference to myths and fairy tales, how there is among men a subconscious fear of the receptivity that characterizes women. Finally, I demonstrated how this subconscious fear has been exercised in the subjugation of women in culture, a domination that strikes primarily at women's receptivity in its widest connotation.

The task now is to explain from a psychological standpoint, the transition from the male fear and awareness of women's receptivity (and of their own lack of it) to the overwhelming emphasis on their own creativity.

COGNITIVE DISSONANCE

One way of doing this is through the theory of cognitive dissonance. This theory maintains that there are limits to the dissonance between expectation and reality that any one of us can sustain. When the limit is approached or reached, certain compensatory mechanisms go to work whose purpose is to lessen the dissonance and bring it to manageable levels.

Let us say, by way of a simple example, that I am invited to two parties on the same day, at the same time, in two very distant places from each other, so that I cannot attend one for a time and then move to the other. Party #1 is given by John and party #2 is given by Michael. I choose to go to one of the parties, the one given by John, but the fear that I may not enjoy myself as much at this one as at the other haunts me and troubles me. That is, a dissonance is created between my expectation of a good time and my choice of John's party as its context. Soon, however, the thought intervenes that John has been a better friend to me than Michael, and that Michael's parties tend to be more rowdy, so that in reality, I stand a much better chance of having a good time at John's than at Michael's. This thought lessens the dissonance and allows me to pursue my choice and enjoy myself.

Philip Slater, who uses cognitive dissonance theory as the foundation for his book *The Pursuit of Loneliness*, comments that "we learned long ago to suspect, when a fear seems out of proportion, that it has been bloated by a wish" (2).

But it is not simply a matter of fear. The mechanism applies equally to hatred, a point Hermann Hesse captures beautifully in *Demian*: "If you hate a person, you hate something in him that is part of yourself. What isn't part of ourselves doesn't disturb us" (95). In fact, the mechanism applies to all intense desires which, for whatever reasons, we feel unable to satisfy. The dissonance is diminished by tainting the desired objects and rendering them, thus, less desirable.

In the case of sexism it is, of course, women's wholeness that men desire but feel unable to achieve, due to their lack of receptivity. To lessen the dissonance, women are demeaned, made less desirable, and what men have (their creativity) is emphasized. There is, thus, an overt fight against, or resistance to, what men inwardly desire. Jeane Baker Miller expresses this same point cogently:

> Freud said that the basic thing that men struggled against is identification with the female, which, a psychoanalyst would immediately have to say, also implies the desire for that identification. I would like to suggest that men struggle not against identification with the female *per se* in a concrete sense, but that men do indeed . . . desire to recapture those parts of themselves which have dreaded and frightening properties for men, but which have been made much more frightening because they have been labeled "female" (Miller, *New*, 46).

While this psychological explanation of the mechanism of sexism is adequate, I believe it can be supplemented by another, especially because sexism entails such a large-scale oppression of, and violence against, women. It is not simple hatred that must be explained, but a real craze.

RESSENTIMENT

The psychological mechanism of the creativity craze must now be explained. It is, of course, the very mechanism of sexism. If it were merely a question of finding a male substitute for the creativity of women, any other creative activity would do. But if it is a matter not merely of devising a male kind of creativity but also, even especially, of avoiding any reference to receptivity and the male lack of it, then the subjugation of women, their relegation to the background in home and public affairs, the over-covering of their bodies with elaborate dress — in short, their violation, becomes understandable. To substitute one creativity for another does not fully explain either war or sexism; to wish to obliterate any trace of receptivity does, for such a cover-up requires force.

The hatred, derision, and subjugation of the female evident in males and in male-dominated society can be understood by reference to the notion of *ressentiment*. It is the theoretical framework of *ressentiment* that explains how the male lack of a distinctive receptivity is eventually turned into sexism.

I use the term here in the meaning given to it by Max Scheler. For Scheler, *ressentiment* is a "self-poisoning of the mind . . . caused by systematic repression of certain emotions and affects which, as such, are normal components of human nature" (Scheler 45). The emotions thus suppressed are those connected with receptivity. The result is envy, which, according to Scheler, "is due to a feeling of impotence which we experience when another person owns a good we covet" (Scheler 52; Dworkin, *Intercourse*, 97). However, the tension between desire and lack does not necessarily lead to envy. Envy occurs when the tension "flares up into hatred against the owner," so that "the latter is falsely considered to be the *cause* of our deprivation. . . . Both the experience of impotence and the causal delusion are essential preconditions of true envy" (Scheler 52).

Envy is especially vicious when the values we lack but covet are such that they cannot be bought or easily acquired; however, they are the type of values in reference to which we compare ourselves to others. Thus, to this envy is added, besides the feeling of lack and of hatred of the possessor, the feeling of powerlessness. This is *"existential envy,"* and it "is directed against the other person's very *nature.*" It is "as if it whispers continually: 'I can forgive you everything, but not what you *are* — that you are *what* you are — that I am not what you are — indeed that I am not you'" (Scheler 52).

Man envies woman her vaginal void. This existential envy sparks ressentiment, and ressentiment leads him to devalue the envied void. Writes Scheler:

> To relieve the tension, the common man seeks a feeling of superiority or equality, and he attains his purpose by an illusory devaluation of the other man's qualities or by a specific "blindness" to these qualities. But secondly — and here lies the main achievement of ressentiment — he falsifies the values themselves which could bestow excellence on any possible object of comparison . . . . When we are unable to attain certain values, value blindness or value delusion may set in. Lowering all values to the level of one's factual desire or ability . . . construing an illusory hierarchy of values in accordance with the structure of one's personal goals and wishes (58-59)—

such are the mechanisms of *ressentiment*. These are the mechanisms, I believe, that account most profoundly for the male delight in war, for the subjugation of women, and for the emphasis on creativity at the expense of receptivity throughout the entire social spectrum.

The origin of this *ressentiment* is to be found, probably, in the power role inversion that characterized the rise of patriarchy. The "virtues" that were extolled for millennia in the matrifocal cultures of the old world — generativity, birthing, artistry, openness, mystery — but which males found so difficult to possess, became the domain of the conquered as Indo-European hordes systematically descended from their lurking northern sites between 6000 and 1000 B.C.E. In contrast, the "slave morality" of men that had silently proclaimed strength, clarity, obviousness (Paglia 22 *ff.*) as virtues was slowly catapulted into prominence and eventually became dominant. The lightning bolt of Zeus or Indra, intermittent symbol both of light and interference, replaced the soft enveloping pallor of the revolving moon; the objective, unavoidable phallus, glorified in the figure of Priapus and other ithyphallic deities, such as Pan, replaced the unobservable and mysterious cave of the Earth Goddess; the smoldering hatred of the male "slave" became the haughty *ressentiment* of the male "master," aided and supported by the conceptualizing male priesthood that had already begun to assert its independence in Mesopotamia, Egypt, and the Mycenaean tribes, among others. Gilgamesh's taunt to Ishtar (Sandars 85-87) is echoed two millennia later by Jesus's prediction of the apotheosis of the meek (*Mat.* 25:31-46) and Tertullian's ringing preview of its sadistic and vengeful fulfillment in the Last Judgment (*De Spectaculis* 29 *ff.*; Nietzsche, *Genealogy* I, 15).

BANALITY

Ressentiment offers a sophisticated explanation of the appearance, rise, and continuation of sexism. But sexism itself, as perpetrated, is a superficial attitude. It requires no deep thinking. Rather, the opposite is the case. Sexist ideology is banal in the extreme, and it is most commonly exercised by those people who think the least or in the most superficial fashion, and who are most unused to dialoguing with themselves, which is part of what thinking is.

In a note on his play *Rhinoceros*, Eugène Ionesco tells a story about de Rougemont's first encounter with Hitler. It was 1938, and he was in Nuremberg, attending a Nazi rally, and waiting for the appearance of the Führer. As Hitler strode down an avenue on his way to the speakers' platform, the huge crowd roared with excitement, and de Rougemont felt swept away by the clapping, the shouting, the frenzy that electrified the people. He was about to join in the shouting when he felt his hair stand on end, as it suddenly struck him that he was in the presence of Evil, capital E, evil personified, yet nonetheless frightening, terrifying (Ionesco xi).

Such an account, as well as the hair-raising reports of cruelty to girls and women, might lead one to believe that Evil, wherever it appears or manifests itself, is huge, enormous, spectacular, overwhelming. But that is not the case. De Rougemont himself comments on the diminutive stature of Hitler as he entered the avenue, and Hannah Arendt, in *The Life of the Mind*, emphasizes the commonplace, almost pitiful character of Adolf Eichmann. No monster here, she says, however monstrous his acts; just the contrary:

> What I was confronted with was utterly different and still undeniably factual. I was struck by a manifest shallowness in the doer that made it impossible to trace the uncontestable evil of his deeds to any deeper level or roots of motives. The deeds were monstrous, but the doer — at least the very effective one now on trial — was quite ordinary, commonplace, and neither demonic nor monstrous. There was no sign in him of firm ideological convictions or of specific evil motives, and the only notable characteristic one could detect in his past behavior during the trial and throughout the pre-trial police

examination was something entirely negative: it was not stupidity but thoughtlessness (Arendt 4).

It is this banality, this ordinariness of evil, that also confronts us in the characters of Kafka's *The Trial* and *The Castle*. Raskolnikov, in Dostoievski's *Crime and Punishment*, is an ordinary student with illusions of grandeur. Merseault, in Camus's *The Stranger*, is about as ordinary a man as one could ever encounter. But this ordinariness does not prevent him from killing an Arab; in fact, it is because of the thoughtlessness of his very ordinary life that he kills, a point that Camus undoubtedly wished to emphasize. Similarly, our presidents, dictators, politicians, and even our policemen, are ordinary human beings who eat, sleep, marry, go to the bathroom, and get divorced like the rest of us. What makes so many of them evil and the originators of evil consequences is not some Satanic or Mephistophelian quality, no overweening pride, no detectable quirk, but their lack of conscience, their lack of inner dialogue with themselves, their lack of self-awareness — their lack of thinking.

Specifically, the evil of sexism is not perpetrated by monsters or perverts (although there *are* monstrous acts committed by individual men); no, sexism is the crime of ordinary people, ordinary men (mostly), who in their ordinariness are unable or unwilling to think, to question themselves, to answer their questions about what their lives are all about.

The mindlessness of sexism is manifest in the use of trite clichés ("women belong in the home," "women deserve it [rape]," and so forth); in the use of bureaucratic language; in the use of language that reveals the speaker's unwillingness or inability to universalize, in the ethical meaning of the term (i.e., to commit oneself to being treated in the same way as one treats others); in the reductionistic character of most sexist utterances ("all they want is power," "when women say No they mean Yes"); in the unwillingness to be informed about what is going on, especially the inconceivable pain that is caused daily by sexism; and so on.

Sexists, the millions of them, are not ogres; they are just ordinary men and it is precisely because sexism is perpetrated by ordinary men, and because ordinary men are the majority, that sexism is so pervasive and so difficult to eradicate.

It is also because sexism is perpetuated by the schooling system, an institution that, from time immemorial, has had enormous influence in shaping the views of men (especially). This topic is explored in some detail in the next chapter.

Chapter 7

Schooling and Sexism

This chapter seeks to pull together some ideas about schooling and its role in the preservation of sexism through the ages. The connection should be obvious: schooling began historically at about the time that human society was changing from being Goddess-centered to being God-centered. It began, too, in the wake of the invention of writing and reading, a revolutionary turn of events that would favor the male element in society.

Perhaps the most important factor in the school's contribution to the perpetuation of sexism lies in the fact that its structure favors male ways of knowing. In previous chapters I referred several times to the differences between men's and women's ways of knowing. Now is the time to do a more thorough investigation of these differences. Therefore I shall begin this chapter with a brief analysis of consciousness. This analysis will lay the foundation for a critique of some elements of the schooling structure, especially reading.

MASCULINE AND FEMININE CONSCIOUSNESS

According to Edmund Husserl, René Descartes' *Cogito* establishes two things: the certainty of the existence of a subjectivity (that is, a consciousness), and the certainty of the existence of an object (that is, the *cogitatum*). Thinking can no more exist by itself without a subject thinking than it can without an object thought.[1]

Put differently, what is revealed apodictically in the *Cogito* is the fact of the relational character of consciousness. What is *not* revealed is *how* the relation is actualized; for example, whether in an analytical or in a contemplative mode, for one may move towards the object or let the object come to one. In short, no exclusive way of prehending the object is revealed in the *Cogito*.

Consciousness entails an object in the same way as a relation entails a term, an *ob-jectum* (a "thrown-in-front"). Writes Husserl: "Without exception, every conscious process is, in itself, consciousness *of* such and such. . . . Conscious processes are also called *intentional*; but then the word intentionality signifies nothing else than this universal fundamental property of consciousness: to be consciousness of something; as a cogito to bear within itself its *cogitatum*" (Husserl, *Meditations*, 33).

In *Ideas* (#84), Husserl defines intentionality as "the unique peculiarity of experience 'to be the consciousness *of* something'" (223). Then he goes on to say that intentionality is always discoverable in experience, whereas directedness towards the object or away from it need not be so. Intentionality, therefore, in his words, is like an "objective background." Clearly, for Husserl, this "objective background," this "of-ness" of consciousness is nondirectional; it is *neutral* as far as movement towards or away from. Intentionality means *only* "of-ness." From this perspective, relationality is a better term, since it implies no direction.

The relationality of consciousness means that to be consciousness is to be related to an object. Thus, relationality is a transcendental aspect of consciousness. This relationality is not predicamental or accidental, but inherent and essential, so that a distinction between consciousness and its relationality would be only logical and not real. "Of-ness" is not just essential to consciousness: it is constitutive.

It is important to keep this property of consciousness in mind because contemporary studies of women and men (as we shall see below) show that, because of the different effects nurturing has on them, men's consciousness is more "objective," while women's is more "subjective." Such a dichotomy is wrong. Using language more accurately and carefully, one should be saying that men's consciousness is more *separative* and women's consciousness more *inclusive*, while being, at the same time, *objective*. After all, both inclusion and separation involve an object.

Another way of saying this is that, to be related to an object is *ipso facto* to be different *from* it. Therefore there are in all relations (and therefore in all consciousness in so far as consciousness is relational) two modes, *towardness* and *fromness*. These modes, I should iterate, are modes of relationality, not motion modes. If anything is related, in being related to something it is equally different *from* it. This obtains regardless of the action that gives rise to the relation. *Towardness* and *fromness* are both constitutive and constant.

Now, it should be noted that these modes do not depend for their existence on our being aware of them. But they are not, either, a merely logical requirement. They are prereflective; that is, they are implicit in the *ofness* that is the relationality of consciousness. To be directly conscious of an object is to be simultaneously and prereflectively aware of the *ofness* of consciousness as well as of the fact that the object is *not* the consciousness itself *nor* the world in general, while being prereflectively conscious of this very *not*ness; it is like looking at an object which is not the looking itself while being prereflectively aware of the fact that the object looked at is not the subject looking, nor the looking itself, nor the world in general.

While the *cogito* reveals only the fact of relationality, this relationality that *is* consciousness exists in fact as this or that type of relation, and therefore as this or that type of consciousness. In *Cartesian Meditations* (#14), Husserl clearly states that the relation of *cogito* to *cogitatum* admits difference. Thus, there are perception, memory, fantasy, judgment, and so on, all of which are modes of relation to the object — even to the same object. In Husserl's example, I can perceive a house, or remember it, fantasize about or imagine it, make judgments about it, and so on. In all these instances, the essential truth of the relation of *cogito* to *cogitatum* is verified, though differently. In other words, one may be conscious *of* the same object in different manners, which represent different modes of consciousness or of what it means to be conscious.

An analysis of these secondary modes reveals that some of them are more directly or actively inquisitive while others are more actively receptive. It is my contention that the actively inquisitive modes are characteristically masculine while the actively receptive ones are typically feminine. This, of course, requires further elucidation.

So far I have used the term "active" without defining it. The meaning is not far to find. By "active" I mean simply the aliveness of consciousness, the fact of its being the consciousness of a living being. According to this meaning, then, there are two fundamental modes of human consciousness, active-active and active-passive. To be active-active is to act knowingly on something; to be active-passive is to let one be acted upon by something. No human, except when dead, can be acted upon in a purely passive way. Live human passivity is an activity that undergoes activity, an activity that allows or lets itself be acted upon by another.

Besides being intentional or relational, then, all consciousness is active and knows itself prereflectively to be active. That is, all consciousness is prereflectively an encounter with or presence to an object. But this active encounter may be colored by the possibilities of investigating the object, analyzing it, manipulating it; by the possibilities of merely being present to it, wondering at it, or escaping from it; by the possibilities of absorbing the object, engulfing it; or even by the possibilities of letting oneself be analyzed or absorbed by the object (which may be, at least in some ways, a subject). This last mode is possible due to the facticity of all human consciousness.

To be more precise, then: besides being intentional and generally active, consciousness is *active-active* and "directional" or "positing" when it is:

1. *manipulative* in its stance, that is, constructive or destructive, experimental, analytical, or investigative;
2. *suppositional*, analyzing, calculating, or experimenting inwardly with its object; or
3. *aversive*, introversive, being apprehensive, fearful, or escaping its object.

On the other hand, consciousness is *active-active* and "presentive" or "nihilating" when its stance is:

1. *assimilative*, either in a

a. *static* way, in being open to its object, merely seeing or contemplating it, or letting it be; or in a
b. *dynamic* way, when appropriating it, ingesting, absorbing, sucking, or embracing it. Further, this stance may be
2. *accommodative*: that is, either
a. *tensive*, when the mode is perception, insight, intuition, observation, and understanding; or
b. *pensive*, when the mode is wonder, fantasy, thinking, meditation, or contemplation.

Active-passive modes are the obverse of these and are not pertinent to this discussion. In all instances, the mode depends on the nature of the real foundation of the relation that is consciousness. While *all* foundations of the relation that is consciousness imply activity and *ofness* (to/from), the modes of activity are multifarious, as detailed above.

Now, as I have stipulated before, it is my contention that the active analytical modes of consciousness are more characteristically male, while the active presentive/receptive modes are more characteristically female. The reason for this assignation is the very physiological or anatomical constitution of men and women. The connection between anatomy and the modes of consciousness will be explicated later. Here my purpose is to show that there are, indeed, modes of consciousness that are distinctly creative or intromissive, while there are some that are receptive.

But how can I, a man, know this? If my contention is true, a phenomenological analysis of consciousness done by a man would tend to yield only the partial data applicable to men. The objection is valid, but there is a subterfuge. Inference must complete the picture for women.

There is a classical parallel here. Carl Jung wrote: "Since the anima is an archetype that is found in men, it is reasonable to suppose that an equivalent archetype must be present in women; for just as the man is compensated by a feminine element, so woman is compensated by a masculine one" (*Collected Works*, IX. 2, 14). It is obvious that Jung could not have experienced the animus in women directly. His description of the female animus is, therefore, "from the outside," and more an inference than an experience (Wehr 13).

My contention that active-receptive consciousness is typically female is also largely inferential, but the data in support of this allocation are plentiful. I will here deal only with the more relevant ones.

SEPARATION AND CONNECTION

Some data support the existence of two modes of consciousness, one dependent on the development of the male's identity through *separation* from the mother, the other arising from the delineation of the female's identity through *connection* with the mother. A man's consciousness, therefore, would be more inclined/conditioned to approach its object as separate, investigating and analyzing it, while a woman's consciousness would be more inclined to approach its object in an assimilative, presentive way.

Madeleine Grumet argues that "*what is most fundamental to our lives as men and as women sharing a moment on this planet is the process and experience of reproducing ourselves*" (Grumet 4, her emphasis). I alluded to this above in Chapter 1, but from a different point of view. Grumet, as well as Dorothy Dinnerstein and Nancy Chodorow, has in mind the fact that the conditions attending the process by which the human species reproduces itself have a significant influence upon the way we, men and women, turn out to be. These conditions affect our sense of ourselves as men and as women; they affect our ways of knowing; and they underlie the prevailing sexism of our civilizations. "From very early," writes Chodorow, ". . . because they are parented by a person of the same gender, girls come to experience themselves as less differentiated than boys, as more continuous with and related to the external object world and as differently oriented to their inner object world as well" (Chodorow 167).

On the other hand, "being male is, in effect, being not like Mom" (Grumet 185). Further, because the boy is perceived as sexually other, the girl is kept closer to the mother. Her experiences, therefore, continue to be more inclusive of "merging," while the boy's are more inclusive of "separation." The result is that, as Chodorow says (174), what is male is what is *not* female, while for the girl, what is female is what is *like* the mother. Boys, in consequence, repress relation *toward* (i.e., they emphasize *fromness*); girls do not.

According to Chodorow and Dinnerstein, the initial relationship of the infant, both male and female, is dyadic — mother-child. The father enters the picture "through" the mother, as a *tertium quid*, constituting a triangle. In some ways, the paternal inclusion is contingent or dependent on the mother, a factor that conditions a (mostly) subliminal resentment in the male. "The paternal compensation for this contingency is to delete the mother, to claim the child, and to be the cause, moving to a two-term, cause/effect model, where the father is the cause and the child his effect" (Grumet 16).

The transition to the triadic stage, with the subsequent dominance of the father, is often ritualized, as in Christian baptism. Until the Reformation (and to this day, for Catholics), baptism was to be administered only by the male priest. Only in extreme circumstances could a deacon or another male administer it. The mother, or another woman, was permitted to administer baptism only if doing so were embarrassing to a man; for instance, when the foetus was in danger of dying, as it was still half-way through the mother's vaginal canal (*Codex Iuris Canonici* [1917] 742.2-3). The male priest becomes, thus, the ("spiritual") father of every child.

In Judaism, circumcision, similarly, is always performed by a male rabbi. But here, further, in so far as circumcision affects only male children, one can detect a male effort to appropriate the boy, especially, to a community of males.

Something along these lines must lurk behind the *Genesis* story of The Binding of Isaac (*Gen.* 22:1-19). The event takes place when Isaac is still a small boy, and shortly after Hagar has been dismissed from Abraham's service. Sarah's complaint about Ishmael (*Gen.* 21:10) is her way of claiming Isaac as *her* son, binding him to herself more than he was before. The episode of the trip to Moriah, then, represent's Abraham's affirmation of his own paternity. Sarah is not mentioned in this story — not even once. The story is totally a man's story. It is *Abraham*'s son that is to be sacrificed. He has total control of the boy, for without this totality, the story would lose its great significance.

Isaac is, of course, spared, but he is saved by his *father* and the *angel* of YHWH, two male figures. Abraham has claimed his son, for himself and for YHWH. He becomes, by that act, the "cause" of Isaac as the continuator of his seed. On Mount Moriah Isaac is reborn, this time exclusively from Abraham, and it is in this guise that he becomes, in turn, a patriarch — that is, not as Sarah's child, but as Abraham's.

Zeus, too, claims Dionysus for himself after Semele is killed by his lightning bolt; Hermes claims the infant Pan; and on the banks of the river Jordan, God claims Jesus as *his* son after he is baptized by John (*Mat.* 3:16-17).

This claiming of the child happens paramountly in school. Schooling is the vengeance of the patriarch; that is one major reason why schooling is male-dominated even though many teachers, especially in the lower grades, are women. Among the Lubavitcher Hasidim, even the women's seminaries are run by men.

Schools claim children for the system, which is patriarchal. And the sooner the better. It is, I think, significant, that as the women's movement has grown in strength, so has the insistence that children be placed in school at ever younger ages. It is as if the system feared it might lose its power to claim the children if they stayed too long under the nurturing care of their mothers.

But it is not merely a matter of domination. Grumet suggests that the deletion of the mother has epistemological consequences for both men and women. The following is a schematic view of the differences.

Men	*Women*
Look at the world in terms of the dyad subject/object	Look at the world in terms of the dyad self/others
Look at themselves as the source of authority	"Experience themselves as mindless and voiceless and subject to the whims of external authority" (Grumet 16)
See themselves as creators of knowledge; receiving knowledge is a weakness	See themselves as receptors of knowledge; creating knowledge is a sin (and Eve was punished for it)

Knowing is sequential; relations are ordinal (cause/effect; high/low) and hierarchical	Knowing is holistic; relations are pluralistic (though they may be unifocal) and egalitarian
Knowing is exclusive (based on the exclusion of the other) and therefore tendentious (either/or)	Knowing is inclusive (based on identification with the mother) and therefore conciliatory (and/and)
Knowing is linear, and life is viewed primarily from a production standpoint (work ——> product = war, carpentry, industry)	Knowing is cyclical, and life is viewed primarily from a reproduction stand-point (labor = mothering, teaching)
Knowing assumes difference until relation is proven (the "null" hypothesis)	Knowing assumes relation until difference is proven
Knowing is concerned with sources and authorship, with documentation (*v.gr.*, the *toledots* of the Bible) (Grumet 33)	Knowing is concerned with meaning and subjective appropriation

This delineation admittedly highlights extremes, and the distinctions get blurry when nurturing of both boys and girls is carried out by *both* parents. Still it provides a general schema of the cognitive differences arising from the present conditions of nurturing.

It should also be clear that the cognitive modes of both parents are pretty much set by the time they initiate nurturing, and are probably more intimately connected with physiological differences, as will be explained shortly. Still, the experience of nurturing reaffirms the direction in which the development of consciousness is going since birth. In Grumet's words, "If the 'other' to whom the biological individual is most closely related is the child, then the definition of subjectivity as that which is identical with myself and of subjectivity as that which is other than myself originates in an experience of reproduction that differs for men and women" (10).

Thus objectivity for the boy is more direct, since it is based on the experience of himself as the "not-feminine," or simply, "the other." For the girl, on the other hand, objectivity is the product of the *tertium quid*, the father. She and her mother make up an intersubjectivity in opposition to which, as object, the father is the "third element," "the other."

Later, after the Oedipal phase, the girl, *not* having had to reject the mother, will see other objects, male as well as female (and neuter), as *alternative* others, while the boy, having had to establish his identity in the negation of the mother, will perceive objects as *substitutes* for the mother. Objective relation, for the girl, will be a matter of choosing among alternatives; for the boy, they will be negatively colored, as are all substitutes for "the *real* thing." In heterosexual relationships, girls will see boys as merely different objects on a plane of equal possibilities; boys, on the other hand, will see girls as sequential substitutes, one for the other. The world of relationships for girls is, thus, horizontal; that of the boys, vertical.

Cognitively, it is not be far-fetched to say that the objective world, for girls, is one of continuities and relationships, while that of boys is one of sequences. The world of girls is primarily intersubjective; that of boys, primarily objective; but we should keep in mind the fact that *all* consciousness is "objective." Relationally, the world of girls is characterized by *towardness*; that of boys, by *fromness*. In brief, "Masculine epistemologies are compensations for the inferential nature of paternity as they reduce pre-oedipal subject/object mutuality to post-oedipal cause and effect, employing idealistic or materialistic rationales to compensate as well for the repressed identification that the boy has experienced with his primary object, his mother" (Grumet 185-186).

Such epistemologies are inferential because they cannot be as directly experienced as the symbiotic one with the mother. They are compensatory in that they are substitutes for the original intersubjective relation with the mother. Finally, they tend to be antisubjective because cognitive dissonance exacts a price as male consciousness is constituted as a substitute for the more natural female (intersubjective) one.

Knowing, for a man, is essentially differential. It is, also, perennially haunted by its renunciation of subjectivity. According to Grumet, "the subject/ object relations that characterize Western science mirror this denial of connection to the world" (Grumet 185). This ghost of sunderings past hovers implacably over the cognitive world men have created.

SEEING AND HEARING

Furthermore, as was pointed out in Chapter 2, research data indicate that males are prenatally (that is, before nurture) predisposed to know the world visually, while females are equally predisposed to know the world auditorily. This is not a matter of exclusivity but merely of emphasis.

Vision and hearing, like the other senses, are simply ways of adapting consciousness to a certain field (Merleau-Ponty 217). Beyond mere neurology, they are specific modes for the bodily consciousness to operate concretely. To see is to envelope, penetrate, manipulate consciously (though prereflectively) the world at a distance; to hear is to receive consciously (and prereflectively) the promptings of the world, also from a distance, though perhaps a nearer one.

The research of William Perry (1970) and Mary Field Belenky *et al.* (1986) supports the association of the visual with the masculine and of the auditory with the feminine. According to Perry, men pass through a sequence of knowing perspectives or "positions." These are: (1) *basic dualism*, that is, basic po-larities, the sundering of the world into right and wrong, light and darkness, and so forth; (2) *multiplicity*, a later stage that develops as the world becomes more complex and a simple dichotomy is insufficient to deal with it; (3) *subordinate relativism*, in which there is an incipient analysis and weighing of opinions; and (4) *relativism proper*, in which the diversity of reasonably defensible views is accepted.

According to Belenky *et al.*, women also pass through stages, but these have different characteristics from those of men. They are: (1) *silence*, in which women experience themselves as mindless and voiceless; (2) *received knowledge*, when they begin to perceive themselves as capable of receiving learning; (3) *subjective knowledge*, when they begin to internalize knowledge and consider it personal; (4) *procedural knowledge*, wherein they learn to apply knowledge and to become "objective"; and (5) *constructed knowledge*, in which they see themselves as capable of creating knowledge.

Without invoking here culture, nurturing, or physiology, it is clear that the male "positions" are the products of cleavages and dichotomies, the result of phallic irruptions upon the world, while the female "positions" are more clearly receptive in kind.

Equally, too, it is clear that the stages of men lend themselves to more visual metaphors, while those of women are concerned with hearing. According to Belenky *et al.*, women speak about themselves in terms of "voice" (speaking and listening): "speaking up," "speaking out," "being silenced," and so on, all of which indicate a verbal concern, the counterpart of the auditory modality. For men, on the other hand, the modality is primarily visual (Belenky *et al.* 18-19).

Needless to say, it is the visual mode that has predominated in our patrifocal cultures. The visual is the standard of evidence. "Seeing is believing," we say. When reports that Jesus had risen from the dead circulated among his followers, Thomas declared he would not believe them "unless I see the mark of the nails on his hands and put my finger in the place where the nails were" (*Jo.* 20:25).

BODY KNOWING

Finally, the connection between active analytical, differential, and visual modes of knowing with masculinity, as well as that between active presentive, continuous, and auditory modes with femininity is based on the anatomy of both men and women. I explained in Chapter 2 how male and female physiology conditions generally our encounters with the world. Because of their different anatomies, men approach the world intromissively, while women do so receptively. There is no question of exclusivity here, only of primary modality.

The grounding of cognitive orientations on anatomy or physiology is important because the body is the only incontrovertible and, in a sense, value-free datum we possess. Other research, such as has been reported above, is extremely important, but it is subject to the variations and vagaries of culture and nurture. Only our sexual bodies give us an independent foundation for the association of consciousness modes with gender. Now, clearly, if our general relationship to the world is based on our anatomical structure, our cognitive interaction with the world is going to be conditioned by our specific physiological form, male or female.

From a purely anatomical point of view, what modes of knowing might be characterized as masculine given the male's somatic intrusiveness? Analysis, objectification, intellectualization — generally, the modes of inquisitiveness. Why? Because, obviously, these are ways of intruding (albeit cognitively) into the world. This cognitive intrusiveness is reflected in the terms themselves and is apparent from a brief etymological analysis of them. Analysis (Greek *ana-*, separation + *lysis*, dissolution) means "to tear in"; objectification (Latin *ob-*, in front + *iacere*, lay + *facere*, to make) means "to cause to lay in front"; to intellectualize (Latin *intus*, into + *legere*, to look) means "to peek in." Obviously, these modes are visually oriented and separative in nature. Similarly, modes of knowing that might be characterized as feminine include assimilation (Latin *ad*, to[ward] + *similare*, to make alike), that is, "to make to look like one[self]"; nihilation (Latin *nihil*, nothing), that is, "to make disappear"; and absorption (Latin *ab*, away + *sorbere*, to suck), that is, "to suck in." These modes are closely aural in nature, and they are integrative rather than dispersive. Generally, feminine cognitive modalities would be characterized by receptivity and openness; in short, by wonder. Generalizing further, one could say that calculative modes of thinking are masculine, while meditative ones are feminine.

These modes of thinking, in turn, give rise to more specific intellectual endeavors which we now characterize as academic disciplines but which were not so circumscribed or named at the beginning. As involvement with the outside objective world in an intrusive manner is masculine, so are modes of thinking that are intimately connected with such an involvement: numerical measurement and calculation, manipulative exploration, observation and analysis of the architectonics of the universe — math, science, physics, history, experimental/behavioral psychology, sociology, and allied enterprises (Paglia 18 *ff.*). Similarly, as involvement with the world in a receptive manner is feminine, so too are the modes of thinking required to render one sensitive to the world and accepting of it: cultivation of the affects, wonder, sensitization to color, sound, texture, movement, and taste — philosophy, literature, and the fine arts.

It may be objected that for these connections to work out, the development of cognitive modes based on a sexual bodily sense must begin very early in life. That is, indeed, the case. In fact, current research indicates that hormone-induced gender predisposition takes place in utero and again during puberty. Further, exploration of one's body — that is, taking stock of one's physical existence in the world — begins in the cradle. Tactile, auditory, visual, and olfactory sensations take place continuously during those early days, months, and years. And even though their effects are not registered and organized consciously into cognitive wholes or schemata, nevertheless they contribute to the preconscious formation of identity, which includes somato-sexual components. Whatever else Freud may not have done, or done wrongly, he surely has made us aware of the importance of prereflective infantile sexuality in the formation of behavior patterns cognitive and otherwise (Van Kaam 232-234; Trebicot 288-295; Freud, "Some Psychical," 243-258).

Again, it may be objected that I am making too much of the connection between somatic sexual differentiation and personal-sexual identity, including the distinctive cognitive modes of relating to the world. But such an objection fails to take into account fully the fundamental cohesiveness of bodily and sexual existence. We are our sexual bodies; our concrete presence to and interaction with the world cannot be bodily without being sexual. Sexual physiognomy, therefore, just as any other bodily dimension, is a constant given in our concrete relating to the world. In so far as it is physiological, sexuality is coextensive with living in the same prereflective way as our whole body is (Merleau-Ponty 169).

My body is the way of my consciousness's being in the world. It is in this sense that one can accept Jean-Paul Sartre's contention that "the body is wholly 'psychic'" (*Being* 374). I am speaking of a prereflective being, of course. The unity that I am is not a unity of two factors constituted separately — a body, on the one hand, and a consciousness, on the other. Rather, it is a unity such that our consciousness is wholly a consciousness that is somatic at the same time that it is a consciousness.

But consciousness cannot be somatic without being sexual. Therefore consciousness is fundamentally sexual. My male body is the way of my consciousness's being in the world. A woman's female body is her consciousness's way of being in the world. This being the case, it is not surprising that the ways of being conscious differ significantly for men and women.

READING AND KNOWING

Schooling (*not* reading) favors the visual over the auditory. Two consequences flow from this favoritism. First, because of this emphasis on the visual, schooling ends up being an additional factor in the formation of male and female consciousness.

Because the infant's sense of sight takes time to develop, cognition (re-cognition) for the infant is first tactile and auditory. Infants respond first to voice, and only later to vision. The primary source of sound (and of touch) is usually the mother. She is recognized through sound and touch. The father enters the picture visually, as the *tertium quid*. The boy seeks his identity through differentiation from the mother, which entails the giving up, even the repudiation, of the structures of early childhood. This means, for boys, the renunciation of sound and touch as "girlish." On the other hand, "girls, permitted to sustain the original identification with their mothers, need not repress sound and touch as significant ways of being attached to the world" (Grumet 140).

Reading comes into the picture at this early stage. In so far as it is visual and sequential, it favors the boy — it even is partly responsible for the sequential character of men's knowing — and it becomes an intrusion into the holistic knowing of girls. It plays, therefore, into the conditions of nurturing that already affect male and female ways of knowing. Because reading is essential to survival in school, it is one more influence differentiating between male and female consciousness.

Superficially, reading appears to be merely a matter of seeing, with the added function the imagination must bring in order for us to make meaning out of what we see/read. But reading is much more than that. Reading is an activity in which the physiological functions of seeing (scanning, etc.) are totally suffused with consciousness. Reading is one of those activities in which we note that our consciousness is totally bodily, and our body is totally consciousness. If there is a noise, "we" are distracted; that is, "we" do not get the meaning as well or as easily. If there is a headache (or a stomachache, or a hang-over) "we" do not understand what we read. Similarly, if "we" are preoccupied, scanning by the eyes will lead to no grasping of meaning. When reading takes place there is no split between body and mind; "we" are totally onened. We are, as Merleau-Ponty says, a "body-subject."

Yet our consciousness cannot be bodily without being sexual, as I explained above. Reading, therefore, is a sexualized activity, just as every other activity we engage in. What is particular and specific about this sexualized activity is that it uses the eyes — it is visual knowing rather than aural or tactile knowing. It is, in other words, fundamentally male.

But — and this is the second point — since schooling favors reading and male knowing, it is sexist. The visual mode, in fact, prevails in school, and solid efforts are made to prevent the auditory and the tactile from gaining an entrance or having any kind of influence, especially in high school.

In school, the look prevails. Students must be looked at all the time; they must be super*vised* (Grumet 111-112). Hearing, on the other hand, the feminine characteristic, is controlled. Students can hear only what the teacher says, not what they want to hear from each other. Only the (father-)teacher's voice matters, and only it is to be the "cause" of the students' learning. Students can speak only when asked, that is, when empowered by the teachers. School, thus, becomes a continuation of the father-controlled home, where children must be *seen* but not *heard*. School creates a culture of silence.

The look is especially damaging to little girls, creating a pattern that often repeats itself into adult life. In John Berger's words, "*Men* act and women *appear*. Men look at women. Women watch themselves being looked at. This determines not only most relations between men and women but also the relations of women to themselves. The surveyor of woman in herself is male: the surveyed female. Thus she turns herself into an object — and most particularly an object of vision: a sight" (Berger 47, quoted in Grumet 113; Neumann, *Fear*, 34).

THE TREE OF KNOWLEDGE

In ancient times, thousands of years before *Genesis*, one of the primary symbols of the Goddess was the tree.   A late (*ca.* 200-300 C.E.) Gnostic document known as "Hypostasis of the Archons," speaks of the first woman turning herself into a tree ("Hypostasis," II.89, in Robinson 154-155) — a beautiful and apt metaphor.   The reason for the symbolic association is obvious: the tree has *within itself* its own means of regeneration.   It fertilizes itself and brings forth fruit.   Curiously, in Latin the names of many trees have a masculine ending but are feminine in gender.   Thus language bears witness to the hermaphrodite.

The tree, like woman, symbolizes infinite regeneration; not immortality, but the cyclical return of life.   In early Sumerian mythology the principle of renewal is in fact symbolized by a man, the son and consort of the Goddess.   An early Sumerian seal (Campbell, *Masks*, III, 14) comprises a tree and two figures.   On the one side sits the Goddess Gula-Bau; on the other, Dumuzi, her perennial son-husband, who dies and is "resurrected" every year.   But Dumuzi has this symbolic power because of his association with the Goddess.   He stands as "Lord of the Tree of Life."   Because of him (because of the Goddess) the tree is called "The Tree of Life."   The tree stands also for enlightenment.   It is the tree of knowing, not just good and evil, but everything.   The tree symbolizes knowing because in its blossoming and its withering, and in its bearing fruit, it "knows" the secret of the seasons of the year, the cycle of death and rebirth.   The tree, thus, stands as the symbol of enlightenment and unending life.   Deborah prophesizes under a palm tree (*Judges* 4:4), and Gilgamesh gains for the people of Uruk the tree of rejuvenation.

In the ancient times, the Goddess reigned supreme.   Her son-brother-consort, (the generic) Dumuzi, was crowned in early Fall; he communed ritually with the Goddess, and was then killed at the end of his year.   His "resurrection" took place as another consort was chosen to serve his year.   At some point, however, Dumuzi abrogated unto himself the power to rule.   When Inanna descended to her sister, Ereshkigal, Queen of the Underworld, Dumuzi showed no concern, happy to become the sole ruler.   But when Inanna returned, Dumuzi was punished.   The Goddess still asserted her power, though there was opposition.   Later on, when Ishtar asked Gilgamesh to become her consort, he refused, mindful of the fate that inevitably would be his at the end of his year.

This refusal is unprecedented.   It would have been unheard of a few generations earlier.   It marks a change in people's attitudes toward the Goddess and her power.   By the time the story of *Genesis* is written down (*ca.* 900 B.C.E.), YHWH is in complete control of the Garden.   He can forbid the Goddess Hawaah (Eve) to commune with the earth, to eat the fruit of her own growing, a growing whose "cause" now he claims to be.   Under his male differentiating intellect (Campbell, *Masks*, III, 106 *ff.*) the one tree has become two, each symbolizing one of the attributes of the Goddess, enlightenment and rejuvenation.   When the Goddess disobeys, she is banned from her own Garden, and YHWH retains control of the Tree of Life, abrogating to himself the power that forever belonged to the Goddess, "the Mother of all the living" (*Gen.* 3:20).

Enlightenment and rejuvenation were matters of experience, not abstract knowing. We know this because abstract knowing, the knowing derived from teaching, had not come into the world yet; so, forbidding the learning of an abstract concept (good and evil) when there was no way to learn it would have been useless. Obviously, Adam and Eve could have had no idea of what good and evil are, for if they had, the prohibition would have been superfluous. Also, the implication of the injunction is, really, "Don't do it" rather than, "Don't know it." In the language of philosophy, what Adam and Eve are forbidden to do is "learn how" or "learn by doing" — that is, learn directly from, by, through the body. The penalty for disobeying is "death"; but what death is, of course, they could not have known.

The injunction has not changed. Woman, says Grumet, generally, and especially in school, is "forbidden to know and teach what she has directly experienced" (Grumet 28). What she has directly experienced that is unique to herself is the receptivity of her womb, the filling of her inner space and her maternal breasts — in short, her receptivity and all that is associated with it.

The interpersonal, the source of her identity and her ways of knowing, as well as a principal part of her nurturing experience, is outlawed from curriculum and teaching. On the other hand, she must know the world from every side, turn it, scrutinize it, lift it out of its context (abstract it). And she must teach everything that comes not out of her primary experience but out of that of men. Both as student and as teacher, the system performs what Jesus once said he would do to Mary: it turns women into men, so they can enter the kingdom of consumption.

In a true sense it may be said that "schooling has functioned . . . to repudiate the body" (Grumet 129), not merely by avoiding it as context, but by relegating it to the periphery — to the *extra*-curricular. The repudiation of the body has been a very effective way of avoiding the receptive. After all, the receptive is grounded primarily on the physiological receptivity of the *yoni*. Ignore the body, and the entire receptive structure, physiology and imagination, are ignored with it.

Further, the emphasis on the visual gets around the body question because seeing can be naively construed as a nonphysical activity. The point is conveyed by the fact that "seers," most of whom have been male, can "see" even when they are blind. The mind can see, and it is this seeing of the mind that schools emphasize above all else.

Plato's "Parable of the Cave" was a parable of seeing. The saints had "visions," and Christianity holds the "beatific vision" — the eternal "seeing" of the Divine Essence — as the employ of the saved in heaven and therefore as the acme of human achievement. In heaven, says St. Augustine, "we shall rest and see, see and love, love and praise. This is what shall be in the end without end. For what other end do we propose to ourselves than to attain to the kingdom of which there is no end?" (*De Civit. Dei*, XXII.30). For that end, we shall have been properly schooled on earth.

THE SYSTEM

All societies have initiation ceremonies especially oriented to boys, and even though a primary goal of them may be to render the boy androgynous — that is, perfect — at the beginning of his adult life, an effect of the initiation is, clearly, the introduction of the boy to the world of the father; essentially, removing him from that of the mother. This effect is continued when initiation turns into schooling, first in Sumer, and then throughout the ancient world. Schooling appears with the invention of writing, which begins in Mesopotamia some seven thousand years ago.

It seems that writing was invented for practical purposes, such as keeping accounts, maintaining records of floods, engineering (temple and boat building), and the promulgation of law. It soon became evident that mastery of writing (and its correlative, reading) was extremely important as a tool for social and financial advancement. The scribe's tasks could be seen as more enticing and easier than those of manual work, but writing was not an easy task to master. Learning a language like Sumerian might include the recognition of as many as seven hundred different symbols, plus "word lists," often in two or three languages, since commerce ranged far and wide. The training required took place in schools (*edubba*) and might last six or seven years.

As the culture of the scribe grew, there developed a companion instruction on trading customs, etiquette, dealings with the rich and powerful, and so forth. The sayings preserved from those early days are generally termed "wisdom" literature, and its remnants come from Egypt, Palestine, and Mesopotamia. Akhtoy's advice to his son Pepi (*ca.* 2240 B.C.E.), the "Sayings of Amen-em-ope" (*ca.* 1290), and the Biblical *Proverbs*, are but a few samples of this vast literature.

Schooling was for boys. Through it they were slowly weaned from the world of the mother and inducted into that of the father. When schooling finally incorporated girls (as it did sporadically in Greek times), its purpose was not changed. Neither has it changed through the years. Schooling is still, even now, clearly directed toward the induction of children, especially boys, into the world of men at work (Grumet 32). This world is ruled by the Puritan ethic of work, which has been the dominant ideology since the founding of the American public school.

In 1871, William T. Harris, superintendent of schools in St. Louis and later U.S. Commissioner of Education, stated that "the first requisite of the schools is *Order*: each pupil must be taught first and foremost to conform his behavior to a general standard." Why? Because a modern industrial society requires conformity to train schedules, to working hours, to punctuality at appointments. The school should create such a conformity by being itself a model of precision and order: "the pupil must have his lessons ready at the appointed time, must rise at the tap of the bell, move to the line, return; in short, go through all the evolutions with equal precision" (Tyack 43). And in 1874, in *The Theory of Education in the United States of America*, a pamphlet coauthored with Duane Doty and cosigned by seventy-seven college presidents as well as city and state superintendents of schools, he wrote that "military precision is required in the maneuvering of classes. Great stress is laid upon (1) punctuality, (2) regularity, (3) attention, and (4) silence, as habits necessary through life for a successful combination with one's fellow-men in an industrial and commercial civilization" (Tyack 49-50). It is impossible to miss the masculine ordering of this Puritan ethic reduced to school policy and practice. Quite clearly, as Tyack remarks, "when educators argued that the educated worker made a better employee, it did not simply mean that he could read directions or was less likely to drink whisky or go out on strike; it also meant in effect that he was properly socialized to the new modes of production, attuned to hierarchy, affective neutrality, role-specific demands, extrinsic incentives for achievements" (Tyack 73).

Compulsory attendance laws, introduced slowly throughout the continent, made sure that every child was subjected to this coopting regimen. Thus, for children and young people, the period between age six and sixteen became increasingly occupied by rigidly prescribed activities oriented toward the job market. This was more so in the cities than in the rural areas, but it was true overall just the same. The most formative years of a young person's life became filled with heterotelic and prescribed activities. In his book, *City School Systems in the United States* (1885), John D. Philbrick describes the purpose of schooling as "the imposition of tasks; if the pupil likes it, well; if not, the obligation is the same" (Tyack 40).

Women, in so far as they constituted the largest number of teachers for nearly a century in America, were in charge of inducting children into the world of their fathers. They worked in hostile territory, and they succeeded at it only in so far as they adopted the policies, practices, and objectives of the patriarchal set-up in which they worked (Grumet 50). They were, for the most part, coopted. Every time there has been a movement of reform, it has been seen as anti-American, as "undemocratic," which is another way of saying "unpatri-archal." The current efforts to "professionalize" teaching carry on unwittingly the same opposition.

The system is currently in hopeless disarray. It has been so for decades. But behind the façade of excuses, there is also the undeniable fact that a masculine or patriarchal system cannot deliver what it promises — it cannot be a mother-father, a vaginal procreator. No matter how hard it tries, the patriarchal system cannot be the birthing complex that the mother is (and has been). A child placed in school at an early age will wait in vain for the embracing, nurturing touch of the mother (substitute) that would yet allow it an identity of its own. Such a child has to be satisfied with the "fatherly look" of the teacher who, even if she is a woman, looks at the child from the abstract, systemic point of view of schooling, discipline, order, textbooks, blackboards, homework, and recess. In such a context, the child "finds a self in a look that is directed beyond him toward the symbolic order. We gain a self by losing a self, and all subsequent relations with the other are in some way implicated in an attempt to get the self back, to reclaim what was once ours but was returned to us bonded to language, culture, gender, and patriarchy" (Grumet 125).

The failure of the school system is the failure of the fathers, but no one accepts failure easily or willingly. As Grumet writes, "blame is deflected from the men who establish these policies onto the women who teach the children who fail" (Grumet 23). So the schooling reform efforts are typically aimed at teachers: more exams (like the National Teacher Exam), less control, more administrative supervision, less self-determination, and so forth.

SCHOOLING AND READING

Like schooling, reading, too, is associated with the rise of patriarchy. It was initially monopolized by scribes and priests, and therefore connected hieratically with the male god. Judaism and Christianity, the "religions of the Book" *par excellence* (though Islam followed suit), are also the most patriarchal religions ever to grace the earth. On the other hand, the written record of the Goddess religion is very scant.

Reading comes into the world of the child as it moves from the nurturing of the mother to the visual realm of the father. The implications are enormous. Reading comes as the culmination of a long process during which the immediate, simultaneous, and undifferentiated world of the infant is changed into the mediated, sequential, and differentiated world of the child. A world that is real but nameless becomes a world which is real only when named. A world which is simply "world" becomes a world of "this" and "that." And, finally, a world which is normally apprehended in all its simultaneity is transformed into a world in which events follow one another in (often) irreversible succession — as the words on a page (and the pages in a book) follow each other in ineluctable order.

Naming and differentiating begin with language and are consummated in the Ph.D. Sequencing begins with storytelling and achieves its peak with the learning of reading. Reading, perhaps more than anything else, marks the passage to childhood and culture. Equally, it signals the beginning domination of patriarchy.

There is a sense, therefore, in which reading is fundamental to the continuation of the patriarchal culture, since the two are intimately related. And the relation is not a simple matter of content, but, most importantly, of form and structure. The medium is the message.

Similarly, there is a sense in which any other form of communication that interferes with or opposes reading is counter-cultural (antiphallic). Take the case of radio: it is singularly sequential and aural, and only a few tracks of sound can be carried simultaneously — for example, talk with a music background. In this sense, it is closer to the primal voice of the mother. Or take the case of television: it is visual, aural, and (as Marshall McLuhan has said) vicariously kinesthetic. It is, therefore, more holistic, more simultaneous — more of our sensorium is engaged at the same time, and especially those senses that have been stimulated at an early age, touch, hearing, and sight. Television, again, brings us close to the nurturing ambient of the mother. It is, indeed, a glass breast, a "boob tube." Its medium is the massage; perhaps better, the caress. I am not saying that television is a perfect and commendable medium, or that it is, or should be, a substitute for reading (Götz, "Children"). What I am saying is that we have here a countercultural model of what schooling could and perhaps should be if it is to avoid its sexist characteristics.

McLuhan said once that societies have been changed more by the nature of their media than by the content of their communications. One would have to conclude that schooling has had a greater effect on society because of what it has been than because of what it has taught overtly. Its major impact has been as a medium of induction into patriarchal control. Its most profound effect has been the perpetuation of sexism; and not because of the chauvinism of its administrators and textbooks, but because of its very structure.

For centuries, the image of the school teacher has been that of the guide directing the child's gaze toward the heights of knowledge to be attained. This picture is gentler than that of the old master/mistress with stern face and (phallic) cane in hand. But both are still patriarchal metaphors.

Another picture is possible, that of groups of people, male and female, children and adults, jointly and comfortably wondering at the beauty of unimaginable sunrises. The picture includes parents celebrating because their child brought home an "A" in art, and commencement exercises in colleges and universities in which the achievements of the body are celebrated as much as those of the mind; where wonder is valued as much as analysis; and where the ideal of the educated person is the androgyne.

NOTE

1. Aristotle also states that thinking and perceiving are alike (though different in other ways) in that "in one as well as in the other the soul . . . is cognizant of something which *is*" (*De Anima*, III.3 [427^a 21]). The same is implied by Aristotle when he says that the mind as such is mere potential to know. The mind exists only as thinking takes place, i.e., as an object is thought (*De Anima*, III.4 [429^a 23-24]). It exists (*est actu*) only when actually related to an object. To think is to be actually related to an object of thought.

This same point is stated explicitly by Nâgârjuna: "[There is] no object of knowledge unless it is being known. But the knowing consciousness does not exist without [its object]. Thus you have said that knowledge and the object of knowledge do not exist by own-being [i.e., independently]" (*Lokâtîtastava* 10). Our consciousness, therefore, is always relational — i.e., conditioned, using Nâgârjuna's term.

Berkeley's *esse est percipi* (*The Principles of Human Knowledge*, 3) is counterbalanced by *cogitare est percipere*.

Chapter 8

Technology and Gender

"In a way," Fernand Braudel writes, "everything is technology" (I, 334). Indeed, there is hardly an area of life in which tool-aided tasks are not significant. No wonder, then, that when women are excluded from certain technological domains, they feel that their lives have been adversely affected, that their progress and self-development have been jeopardized. If to get where one needs to go one needs a car, and the car is denied, one's need is thereby denied.

Studies have shown that contemporary women are not as attracted to or as immersed in technology as men. Fewer women are interested in or play computer games, though more women than men slave in factories soldering computer boards; and the "sweat shops" that have been the blight of industrialized societies have employed mostly women and children.

These and similar facts are readily available to all, but they do not tell the complete story of the relationship between gender and technology. This is the case partly because most histories of technology have been written by men, but also because many subtle factors lurk below the surface, or must be looked for and found in what one author called "the underside of history."

TECHNOLOGY

Animals and things have no space within themselves, no distance between their selves and their physical essence, because they have no reflective selves. They are what they are, nothing else. But because humans are not identical with their essence (they can always aspire to more than they are), they appear as a kind of "project" to be actualized through their actions. "Our life is pure task," writes José Ortega y Gasset ("Meditación," V, 341), but task about which we have to think. The use of the brain for making tools or planning tasks is properly *téchnê*, and the understanding of this, its *lógos*, is technology.

Aristotle defined *téchnê* as "capacity to make involving a true course of reasoning" (*Nic.Ethic.*, VI, 4 [1140ᵃ 10]). *Téchnê* is not mere production, or production following instinct (as in the case of bees making a hive), for it involves generalizations; further, it may aim not just at usefulness in a narrow sense, but also at satisfaction — for example, in the making of musical instruments and the creation of paintings and ornaments.

For the most part, without technology there could be no task, and without task *human* life could not exist. This is why, as Ortega put it, "human life begins where technology begins" ("Meditación" 342).

Now, it so happens that a recent discovery in Ethiopia has placed the use of tools by an as yet uncatalogued species of our genus *Homo* around 2.6 million years ago (Menon 34). The significance of this find for us is not so much that tools were *used* at such an early age in the development of our species as that such tools were *manufactured*, which would seem to indicate a rather sophisticated and peculiar use of thinking. As tools became more diversified and complex over thousands of years, brain size doubled and the canine teeth became smaller, for some of their use was being supplanted by the tools (Washburn and Moore 123, 166-167[1]). This would seem to indicate that the kind of knowing that was aborning was at least partially instrumental — we could say technological — because the basic problems of tool *making* were, and are, intellectual rather than motor (Washburn and Moore 74): they involve knowledge of what the tool is good for based on previous experience. As this thinking continued apace and grew more sophisticated, a new dream animal was appearing on the scene, but the dreams behind its expanding foreheads were, to some extent at least, dreams of know-how.[2]

Later, but still at quite an early stage, we find that technology was not exclusively concerned with mastery of the environment and survival, but also with quasi-decorative modifications of the human body for sexual emphasis (circumcision and subincision), self-expression (ear and nose rings, necklaces, tattoos), or group identification (body paint and dress). Evidence comes from as early as the Mousterian culture some 125,000 years ago (Mumford 81). Then, by 45,000 years ago we have evidence that weaving had been invented; we have artistic carvings, the paintings in the caves of Lascaux, Altamira, Nerja, and Chauvet, and the extraordinary so-called Venus figurines — all of which involved technology (Pfeiffer; Yebenes; Chauvet).

It is impossible to tell whether at this stage tasks were apportioned by gender, but at least it can be said that women as well as men had their brains wired for technology. Whatever differences may have appeared later between men and women with regard to technology, it was certainly not due to ability or the lack thereof, but to circumstances of time, place, and opportunity. Thus, when Elizabeth Wayland Barber claims that it was virtually always women who produced textiles, the implication is not that women were weaker and less adept at the tasks of hunting, but that, in the social milieu of the first settlements, weaving was more compatible with childrearing than with hunting, and therefore it became women's task (Barber 12, 29-30). For the same reason, it may have been women who developed horticulture, while men concentrated on agriculture

(Barber 75-76). The point is that any differences between men and women with regard to technical activity must be presumed to have originated in social practice rather than in capacity or the lack thereof.

The process of manufacture begun almost three million years ago must have involved males as well as females. There is no reason why it should not have, and the example of primates confirms this. As humans eventually appeared, we must assume that men and women similarly possessed essentially the same capacity for practical thinking and tool making. The fields or areas where they have exercised this capacity, however, have developed differently as social conditions favored one or the other — with the sole exception of childbearing, a task which was, and has remained, within the exclusive domain of females.

REPRODUCTIVE TECHNOLOGY

The most fundamental instrumentality in the world is reproduction, the engorging of the womb in pregnancy and its forceful expulsion of the live foetus into the world. Making new human life appear through the instrumentality of her own body is the primary technological achievement, and it is woman's prerogative.

In general, human productivity is an extension and universalization of female productivity. Even before humans made stone tools, skirts, and ivory beads, women had children. In fact, as was pointed out earlier, men probably made war in order to appropriate to themselves some of the awesome power of maternal productivity (Noble, *World*, 282; Huston, "Matrix," 126). Ancient Greek women understood this when they joked about denying sex to their husbands in order to put a stop to the Peloponnesian War (Aristophanes, *Lysistrata*); and Roman wives slipped out of their husbands' beds a couple of times a year in order to thwart the law that made them their husbands' property.

The pressure for men to subsume women's productivity and enlarge their own work sphere goes back thousands of years, but it intensified when Christianity pushed celibacy on its clergy beginning in the fifth century. Women had been giving birth indiscriminately to boys and girls, even to the men who became priests; and by managing the priests' households as wives and, later (as celibacy began to be enforced), as housekeepers and concubines, they produced the wherewithal required for priests to subsist and do their work. This change was hardly noticed, because, in general, women were doing everything that men did, from salting pigs to cooking and baking, tilling, spinning, and weaving, as is evident from the illuminated mediaeval miniatures illustrating women's work. But the slow exclusion of women through celibacy, especially in the monasteries, required the priests to become self-sufficient, which meant the appropriation by men of the productive activities of women in the home. In the monasteries, men cooked, cleaned, and generally kept house, as women had done before for them; they even gave (spiritual) birth through baptism; and in so doing, they trespassed with impunity into the territory traditionally assigned to women. Auguste Comte generalized this transition when he wrote to John

Stuart Mill in 1843: "The natural movement of our industry tends gradually to pass to men the professions long exercised by women" (quoted in Noble, *World*, 283).

Mythology had already revealed men's urge to appropriate to themselves the power of childbearing, the ability to "make" humans. Zeus gestated Dionysus and Athena, Prometheus (and, among the Hebrews, Elohim) created the human race, Eve was born of Adam, a rabbi made a *golem*, and, more recently, Dr. Frankenstein invented his "creature." Today men make robots which are, after all, substitute human beings; and it is the same with cloning. One of the undiscussed issues with cloning is not so much that men are playing God as that they are playing women. As David Noble remarks (*Religion*, 286), *in vitro* fertilization, cloning and robotics are all steps toward the creation of artificial wombs for men. Put differently, they are efforts to masculinize the reproductive technologies of women.

CONTRACEPTION AND ABORTION

In a sense, masculinization is an extreme; it is a transparent effort to substitute men for women. An intermediate step has been the control of women's reproductive powers by turning the private technology of reproduction into the public domain and invoking laws against contraception and abortion (Illich 75-76). The womb has become public territory.

Since the rise of patriarchal societies there has been a tendency among rulers to control a woman's womb by extolling virginity, legislating the accepted forms of intercourse and marriage, and, more recently, forbidding contraception and abortion. The same powers that controlled production have sought to control reproduction. Laws regulating intercourse and marriage appear as far back as the Code of Hammurabi (*ca.* 1792-1750 B.C.E.). The ancient Greeks and Romans legislated these, too, but they were not particularly concerned with contraception and abortion. In fact, in Rome, the *paterfamilias* retained into the times of the Empire his right to "expose" to death his children after birth. A child was not really "his" until he had picked it up, literally, from the ground where the midwife had placed it. Exposure of newborns was common, even *en masse*. Such practices occasionally sparked concern among the emperors, fearful that too great a decrease in population would cut into the labor force and the army and entice marauding barbarians to invade, but rather than forbid abortion and exposure, celibacy was forbidden — for instance, by Augustus (Suetonius, "Augustus," 34; Peter Brown, *Body*, 7) — and castration without judicial permit (a male form of contraception favored by Roman matrons) (Juvenal, *Satires*, VI.367; Peter Brown, *Body*, 268) was banned by Domitian and Hadrian (Suetonius, "Domitian," 7; Ulpian, in *Digest* 48.8.4.2).

Christianity, on the other hand, frowned on contraception, abortion, and exposure as sinful. Under its aegis, sexuality was entirely reconceptualized. Intercourse, according to Augustine, was justified solely for the sake of reproduction — that is, for producing people to swell the heavenly ranks of the elect, for Augustine was not concerned with increasing the Roman labor force. "The sexual intercourse of man and woman," he wrote " . . . is in the case of mortals a kind of seedbed of the [heavenly] City" (De Civ. Dei, XV, 16, 3), for intercourse exists and is engaged in "until . . . the number of the predestined should be complete" (De Civ. Dei, XIV, 10). This view made the production of offspring the goal of intercourse. "Matrimony," he proclaimed, "derives its meaning from this, that a woman marries for no other reason than to be a mother" (Contra Faustum, XIX, 26).[3] St. Isidore of Seville, the first Christian writer to talk specifically about the three goals of marriage,[4] put it this way: "There are three reasons for the sake of which a man takes a wife: first for the sake of offspring . . . second, for mutual help . . . third, because of sexual desire" (Etymolog., IX, 7, 27), meaning by the last one that marriage was a remedy for lust. Some five centuries later Peter Lombard summarized the tradition by stating that "the final and principal reason for entering marriage is the procreation of offspring" (Sentent., IV, d.30, c.4). Aquinas concurred (Summa Theol. I, 98, 1), projecting this rationale into the succeeding centuries. In so far as contraception and abortion violated the end of intercourse thereby depleting the ranks of the elect, they would have to be avoided. Failure to comply led to sin. The penalty for sin was hell. The control of reproduction was achieved through fear of hell.

This view becomes crucial during the formative years of modern capitalism which witness also the rise of rationalism in science and philosophy. Hobbes (Leviathan) and Descartes (Discourse, Part V) perceive the body as a machine (Merchant, Chapters 8-12). Such machines are plentiful and readily available to the captains of industry. Thus the rising proletariat become the instruments of capital, their bodies the tools of production, whereas women's wombs are the sources of these tools. Women are, as it were, the subcontractors. Therefore their wombs must be controlled in such a way that they will produce as many living tools as will be needed to maintain production. To achieve this, heterosexuality must be made the norm[5] while contraception and abortion must be eliminated, not merely as sin, but also as economic waste. The capitalist state, not just the Church, has a stake in this. At a time when the Church sees its influence waning, it discovers in the secular realm, in nascent capitalism, a powerful ally to enforce its control of the womb. Further, and more recently, it makes a new ally in patriotism, so that having children becomes the patriotic duty of married couples, for without children the large armies required by modern warfare are impossible to muster, and without armies defeat is certain (Ranke-Heinemann 289-294). As a result, contraception and abortion become sinful, unprofitable, unpatriotic, and (until recently) unlawful.

The modern challenges to capitalism (especially, and despite its recent setbacks, that of Communism), and the growing awareness of its defects, shortcomings, inhumaneness, and even moral decay, may be seen as events weakening the hold it and the Church have over the working man's body and the woman's womb, and calling for immediate reform. At the same time, the rise of feminism (that is, of the owners of the womb) appears as part of the broad effort to reconsider and perhaps restructure the very economic and militaristic fabric of democratic capitalism. In this context the debate about abortion, with its emphasis on the woman's right to decide even against Church, state, Wall Street, and the Pentagon, is symptomatic of what might be called the feminine proletariat's[6] fight to wrest a measure of self-control from the forces of patriarchal capitalism, much as modern unionism has marked a similar struggle to win from the bourgeois capitalists at least a modicum of dignity and control.

TECHNOLOGY AND GENDER

Ivan Illich claims that people have always been aware of gender and structured their social arrangements according to it. We have no evidence from prehistoric times, but since the Paleolithic, there are clear signs that gender awareness existed — for example, in the Venus figurines and the cave paintings. This evidence multiplies during the Neolithic, and it is reflected in language once writing appears. Besides the obvious male and female genders in the vernacular, there is also a neuter one which seems to apply to certain specific objects, varying from culture to culture as to its specificity.

In gendered societies there exists a complementarity of labor that apportions particular tools and tasks to each gender without necessarily creating a hierarchy.   There are taboos about crossing boundaries and using or even touching the tools of a gender other than one's own, but an implicit assumption seems to be that the good and prosperity of the gens depends on both genders keeping to their tasks. In ancient Athens women manage the home and the temple, while men manage the *polis*, and so men are citizens, and women are not. Tasks such as weaving seem to be traditionally female, while tasks such as hunting and waging war seem to be traditionally male (*Iliad*, VI.443); and spindle and loom are taboo to the men just as bow and arrow and sword are taboo to the women. Both, however, are essential to the preservation and welfare of the family, the clan, and the society. As far as we can tell, while the tools of technology are apportioned differently to men and to women, successful execution of tasks by each gender is necessary for the thriving of the clan. Women are praised for doing their best at their tasks, and so are men — for example, the *Odyssey* (VII. 108-111) says of the Phaeacians that their women are known to be the best weavers, while their men are the best sailors; and the fact that *we today* may view such womanly tasks as inferior is merely an anachronistic judgment. Thus, the praises of woman sung in *Proverbs* 31:10-12, 26-31 may strike us today as condescending and chauvinistic, but they represent what that society considered that gender's excellence, while the attributes of the heroes given in the *Iliad* reflect what that age considered outstanding in the male gender.

One could say that, at that time, and in those societies, the differences in tasks between men and women, and the taboos against the use of tools belonging to others, were irrelevant, for the concern was not with individuals, or with one gender lording it over the other, but with the preservation of the whole. No concerted individualism seems to have existed, and the principle of distributive justice, as elaborated later by Plato, seems to have governed the apportionment of resources. But these conditions did not last forever.

One senses in the defacement of Hatshepsut's records an effort to delete the memory of the (woman) Pharaoh who ruled Egypt like a man, even in dress and head gear, while her stepson/nephew sulked. Some people must have found her reign an intolerable usurpation of a man's ruling tasks, and her touching of the sacred vessels a desecration of men's ritual tools. In Greek literature, too, we note the disturbing presence of the Amazons, and also, that a certain insidiousness has crept into the estimate of women's tasks. Agave refers to this explicitly (*Bacchae* 1190 *ff.*), and so does Medea (*Medea* 460 *ff.*). Later, the Pauline letters strain to keep women "in their place" (*1 Cor.* 11:3; *1 Tit.* 2:11), while making the case (argued by Plato before) that a well-ordered society requires each to perform his/her tasks without envy of others (*Rom.* 12:5).

According to Illich, by the Middle Ages, there began to be a movement toward standardization of certain ordinary tasks beyond those enshrined in the guilds. This would account for the fact, mentioned above, that the pictures of women in illuminated manuscripts depict them as employed in essentially all the tasks that were generally performed by men. Together with this standardization, there appeared in language a certain vocabulary that eliminated the traditional gender distinctions. When both men and women are referred to as "citizens," as "persons," as "human beings" (though the male term *homo* is used for both), a new genderless vocabulary appears, and with it, the notion that tasks and tools are also genderless, and therefore should be indiscriminately available to men and to women.

Illich suggests that this unisexism took place in the name of economic progress, for, he says, "an industrial society cannot exist unless it imposes certain unisex assumptions: the assumptions that both sexes are made for the same work, perceive the same reality, and have, with some minor cosmetic variations, the same needs" (Illich 3). Scarcity breeds competition for the jobs which have been redefined as unisex or genderless, and which therefore are supposedly available to all. But genderless humans are an abstraction, so the whole enterprise of complete equal access is doomed to failure.

Illich's point is that the elimination of vernacular gender and the invention of the abstract, genderless "human," were thought necessary to the pursuit of economic and political equality conceived in more individualistic terms. It also was — and still is — an effort to perceive people in a generalized way that would get beyond accidents of color, nationality, language and — yes — gender, offering all indiscriminate access to the goods of society. But in the public realm, such equality has not been achieved, and it is debatable whether it can be achieved at all, because differences cannot be obliterated by political or philosophical decree. Gender, especially, cannot be eliminated. In older societies, gender allowed a distribution of tools and tasks that empowered each and every one, man and woman, in their respective spheres, but the neutrality of nongendered reality has created a no one's land where the more powerful reign and women are subdued (Illich 71).

This is an important root of the frustration experienced by women when they are cut off from technological and other jobs to which they feel entitled by the mere fact of being human and of being citizens. There is an ambiguity here, because, on the one hand, we are all human, but, on the other, we are all gendered. The *fact* of citizenship (much less the *concept* of humanity) cannot eliminate the *fact* of gender; concretely, the fact that women can give birth and men cannot. One must wonder, then, whether the push for equality in which men have allowed, and even encouraged, women to engage is not another kind of smokescreen designed to prevent women from looking at what is *really* going on. The pursuit of unisex equality must at some point appear suspiciously for what it is, a desperate attempt by men to avoid confronting the gender question, and with it, the reality of the female womb.

This does not mean that women should abandon their efforts to have access to tasks of their choice in which they believe their human potential will be realized. It *does* mean that such pursuits should be based on the principle of justice, not equality.

In the Middle Ages, some Christian theologians claimed that women would be resurrected as men, for only men are worthy of eternal life. This is the ultimate equality, to be subsumed into some one else's existence. Aquinas disagreed, explaining that, at the resurrection, men and women will rise as separate but equal genders, the only difference among individuals being merit (*Summa Theol., Supplem.* 81, 3 *ad* 2); and this view prevailed, though you would not know it from the opposition to women priests. At any rate, the point, according to Aquinas, is the just but unequal allocation of reward. The same should apply to the relationship between technology and gender.

NOTES

1. In the human brain, the area for hand skills is very large, far larger than in any ape, with the thumb occupying a disproportionate space.

2. Without the data we possess today, Karl Marx and Friedrich Engels had already concluded that "the first *historical* act of these individuals distinguishing them from animals is not that they think, but that they begin *to produce their means of subsistence*" (*The German Ideology*, I, 2). See also Engels, "The Part Played by Labour in the Transition from Ape to Man," and Eiseley, *The Immense Journey*, Chapter 8.

3. In another passage Augustine writes: "The birth of children is what you most abhor in marriage, and thus you turn your 'hearers' [adherents] into adulterers of their own wives, when they are on the alert [for the infertile period] to see that their wives do not conceive. . . . They wish to have no children, *for whose sake marriages are contracted*. Why then do you not forbid marriage altogether . . . if you take away what constitutes marriage in the first place? For if that is taken away, husbands are shameful lovers, wives are harlots, marriage beds are brothels, and fathers-in-law are pimps" (*Contra Faustum*, XV, 7, emphasis added). This is, of course, a condemnation of the "rhythm method," which yet is sanctioned by the Catholic Church today.

4. There were precedents in the Roman world. Musonius Rufus claimed that sex

for its own sake was immoral, and Seneca, writing to his mother Helvia, maintained that "sexual desire was given to humans not for enjoyment, but for the propagation of the race" (*ad Helviam*, XIII, 3; Ranke-Heinemann 12-13).

5. With the rise of patriarchy comes the advent of heterosexuality and (re)production as the norm, commanded by the Bible's God (*Genesis* 1:28 and 2:24-25).   First impressions suggest that gays and lesbians merely subvert the sex/gender system, but they also threaten capitalism (Stein 38; Rubin).

6. By using this expression I do not mean to take a position on the issue whether or not women are a *class*, economic, racial, sexual, or social.   I simply wish to emphasize that the issue of abortion, in so far as abortion impacts on capitalism, extends well beyond the ethical and the religious bounds.

Conclusion

The arguments have been presented, the data have been analyzed. The point now is to achieve closure. However, before the leave-taking there is an issue that must be clarified so as to preclude misunderstanding. It concerns the relationship between sex and gender, between our somatic endowment and what we do with it, between our being born male or female and our becoming men or women.

PHYSIOLOGY AND CHOICE

Throughout this book I have claimed that there is a physiological ground to our sense of what is masculine and feminine. Bodily sexual identity is a yardstick for gender beyond the relativity of culture. Without this yardstick, all social criticism of sexism becomes eventually ineffectual (Götz, "Masculine/ Feminine," 25, note 5; LeVay 131). But the emphasis on physiology revives a specter that haunted the early part of this century and that roamed even the societies of Plato and Aristotle. This is the belief that anatomy is destiny. I do not advocate this position, nor does it seem to me to be a corollary of the moderate essentialism that underlies my thesis.

Physiology is an incontrovertible datum, but it is not the whole question. Physiology, as Maurice Merleau-Ponty says of the body, is "the barest raw material of a genuine presence in the world" (165; LeVay 108); it represents the concrete possibility of being present in the world, but it is realized only through the actual choices we make to become men and women. Anatomy, therefore, is not destiny; choice is.

Everything we become is concretely our own doing. The living of a certain life, the behaviors, the inclinations, become ours upon our acting them out. To claim otherwise would be deliberately to forget that these drives are realized with our consent, that they are not just "forces of nature," but that we lend them efficacy by a perpetually renewed decision concerning their value (Sartre, *Being*, 76). Thus I am not just my sexual body, but what I have chosen to become with my "given" physiological endowment. This choice is not unlike the one each one of us must make, at some point, to accept one's height, one's face, and generally one's physiognomy.[1] Something like this idea must lurk in Friedrich Nietzsche's sub-titling *Ecce Homo* "How One Becomes What One Is." As he himself wrote, "My humanity is a constant self-overcoming" (*Ecce Homo* 233) — that is, a striving to integrate and actualize concretely all the givens in one's own unique endowment.

Not a simple or easy thing, this process of self-actualization. Actualization is no mere freeing of the potential, like letting air out of a balloon; rather it is a process of strenuous construction that often involves, also, destruction and continuous striving, like the work of the waves upon the shore, where the difference is that *we* are both waves and shore. Nietzsche says:

> How greedily this wave approaches, as if it were after something! How it crawls with terrifying haste into the inmost nooks of this labyrinthine cliff! It seems that it is trying to anticipate someone; it seems that something of value, high value, must be hidden there. — And now it comes back, a little more slowly but still quite white with excitement; is it disappointed? Has it found what it looked for? Does it pretend to be disappointed? — But already another wave is approaching, still more greedily and savagely than the first, and its soul, too, seems to be full of secrets and the lust to dig up treasures. Thus live waves — thus live we who will (*Gay Science* 310).

"How one becomes what one is," then, does not mean merely how one actualizes oneself or existentializes one's genetic, cultural, and other inheritance. It means, purely and simply, how one becomes what one is becoming; how one puts together and unifies the multifarious strands of one's living including, of course, one's sexual body.

Thus, even though essential and primary in time, anatomy is not destiny. Each one of us chooses to become a man or a woman. We are born male or female; we become men or women; and a few among us have striven for the fullness of androgyny.

"A SORT OF ART WORK"

All gender is, in some manner, the result of choice. Whether conscious or unconscious, whether influenced by society much or little, we are, as gendered beings, what we choose to become. More, the sexual identity we give ourselves is not something we bring forth truly formed from inside, like a fully grown infant birthed through cesarean section; neither is it something "out there" to be discovered in due course of time, like a treasure hidden in our backyard. Rather, it is something that must be *created*.[2]

This leads Nietzsche to claim that we must be the poets of our own lives (*Gay Science* 299) (understanding "poet" in its original meaning of "maker"), and Friedrich Hölderlin to state that "humans dwell poetically on this earth" (VI, 25, line 32). Martin Heidegger interprets this to mean that "existence is 'poetical' in its fundamental aspect" (282), for it is the function of poetry to create images that contain the invisible in a visible way, something it does through metaphor. Poetic language is not concerned with metaphor for the sake of metaphor, but with metaphor in so far as it is the revelation of what remains essentially unknowable and unrevealed in its totality — in our case, what it truly means to be a man or a woman. Our chosen lives, then, are like living metaphors of the mysterious reality of human gender. To the extent that this peculiar epiphany of the mystery of gender is achieved in song or word, true poetry is created; to the same extent, if willed and created, is human life authentic. Becoming gendered, then, creating ourselves as men and as women, is a sort of artwork (Nehamas 3), and as with all artworks, some may be said to be more beautiful than others, and reasons may be given to support such evaluations.

All choices, *quâ* choices, are equal, however different the styles; they are entitled to the same respect and consideration. Further, no life style is universally valid for all. "'This is *my* way; where is yours?'" Nietzsche answered those who asked him for "the way." "For *the* way — that does not exist" (*Zarathustra*, III,11; *Tao Te Ching* 1), and twenty thousand years of painting clearly demonstrate this. Leonardo's "Mona Lisa" and Van Gogh's "Starry Night" disclose to us aspects of the world which are as valid and important as any that have ever been disclosed, but the world is not thereby exhausted; it lends itself to all kinds of interpretations, all of which carry some truth in them. But this does not prevent some from being more beautiful than others. It is the same with life styles.

"Style," writes Paul Valéry, "signifies the manner in which a man expresses himself, *regardless of what he expresses*" ("Style," XIII, 183). How to evaluate styles? It would seem that those life styles are "more beautiful" which do not strive to impose themselves on everyone, which do not present themselves as universally and objectively valid (that is, which do not pretend to be what they are not), but which, rather, accept themselves as interpretations — living metaphors — while acknowledging the value of others' perspectives and styles (Nehamas 126).

There is, of course, a paradox in choosing one's style while acknowledging the right of others to choose against one's own. But that is the only way in a world that is so immensely rich and multifaceted. The point is to be sincere in one's pursuit, and to choose with the constant awareness that one may be mistaken. In a sense, it must be a choosing without conclusion; that is, a choosing that cannot be demonstrated to be correct syllogistically, either before, during, or after the choosing. This is the reason why there is a dire "night of the soul" at the edge of every choice.

Most importantly, those life styles are most beautiful which affirm (or accept) life in *all* its richness and variety. The question to ask about them, as Nietzsche put it, is, "to what extent it is life-promoting, life-preserving, species-preserving, perhaps even species-cultivating" (*Beyond Good and Evil* 552). This test concerns the styles themselves. But perhaps *the* question to ask is more personal, whether or not one would be willing to choose the same style of becoming a man or a woman all over again if one had the opportunity (*Ecce Homo*, II, 10; *Beyond Good and Evil* 56; *Zarathustra*, III, 2; *Gay Science* 341). And here it is not a matter of choosing only some aspects and discarding others, of staying with the positive and eliminating the negative. If the whole of life (*all* of it) is interrelated, as it appears to be, then any change in any factor or event would have altered any one's life as one has lived it, and one's self as one knows and wills it to be now. Ideally, therefore, the choice of life style would be grounded in the realization that it is impossible to think of oneself as one is now without the past having been what it has been, "and in the effort to become the sort of person who would not even *want*" to have been or acted otherwise (Nehamas 164). This is not unlike what happens in the creation of literary characters: their existence is exhausted by the very narrative that created them, so that the slightest detail cannot be changed without altering the whole (Nehamas 165).

In truth, we are our own novelists. And so it may be possible to understand, choose, and live our gendered styles as literary artworks.

EXIT

Men have no distinctive somatic receptivity, no vaginal void. This lack is obvious, and the efforts to obliterate awareness of it, still more obvious. These efforts are at the root of much of sexism and violence against women, including pornography (Turley 93; Dworkin, *Woman Hating*, Part II). For whatever the effects of pornography may be, one of them at least is this: it offers an imaginative or vicarious outlet to *ressentiment*.

The data I have presented in support of this hypothesis are sufficient to substantiate at least the suspicion that some sort of existential envy underlies sexism, much though we may wish to deny it. And it won't do to say that the incidence of male homosexuality undermines my thesis, for my contention is that men lack a *distinctive* somatic receptivity, not any receptivity at all. Neither will it do to say that the average heterosexual at a porno peep show would be startled by the question, "Do you envy female receptivity?" The value of a hypothesis such as the one presented here hinges on the fact that it unearths unconscious motivations behind the occurrences of everyday life.

Camille Paglia writes: "Nature cares only for the species, never individuals" (10), and she finds this humiliating. I would say "humbling." But I would add that we are *not* just nature. Or, better, we are a different kind of nature, *self-conscious* nature. We are that through which nature knows it cares. But this "through which" is individual. Therefore nature cannot know itself as caring without the individual. This means that, in effect, nature does not care *only* for the species. The flaw in Paglia's account is the failure to see how nature is human and the human natural (Marx), but *not identical*. In this respect her work is reductionistic.

If woman is nature and nature is earth, then death is a return to earth — or a return to woman. Intercourse is a return to woman, but also to nature and to earth: it is a "small death" — *petite mort*, the French term for orgasm. Men fear woman's hole as they fear "the hole in the ground" that is to be their resting place (Paglia 16) — hence the supreme importance that Christ conquer death (that is, woman), and rise again, eternally erect, reassurance against castration.

Ressentiment explains the mechanism of sexism, and schooling practices see to its perpetuation. But in the negativity of *ressentiment* one must discern an affirmation underlining it. Despising in others what one secretly covets means affirming the value of what is despised/coveted; otherwise we would not care. "Sour grapes" comes *after* desire (Camus 17-19; Miller 46). Thus, and despite itself, the subjugation and humiliation of women because men covet what they are (and what men lack) is *ipso facto* the affirmation of the value of what men lack (what women are). It is, as Sartre says of bad faith, *evanescent*. Sexism, therefore, in its very negativity, reveals the seeds of its own elimination and points the direction in which this elimination must move: the search for the male-female, vaginal father (Brown 71); the quest for true androgyny.

Paglia maintains that androgyny "belongs to the contemplative rather than the active life" (21). She means that androgyny is an unattainable ideal. She means, also, that androgyny has been redefined so that in practice it means now that "men must be like women and women can be whatever they like" (22). But this is a downsizing of androgyny that must not be tolerated.

I need not repeat here what I wrote elsewhere about androgyny (*Creativity* 119-128), but merely that androgyny transcends all that is peculiar to only one sex and to mere amalgams of male and female characteristics, whether physical (hermaphroditism) or behavioral. In June Singer's words, "the androgyne is a *representation in human form of the principle of wholeness*" (275). Surely, the *models* of androgyny have tended to combine male and female, whether in shape or story. Some Hindu statues are clearly half male and half female (*ardha-nârîshvara*), and the stories of the transformation of Teiresias into a woman and back into a man may be cited as examples. But these are *symbols* of what remains to be achieved.

There is certainly a mystical dimension to the achievement of androgyny, but this must not be thought to be merely a fruitless kind of meditation, the action of dilettantes and sycophants. Rather, it is the contemplative immersion in an ideal out of which there may eventually be an overflow into the *praxis* of everyday living. For "the way is long and obscurely mystical at the end of which Ch'ien (*yang* [the Creative]) and K'un (*yin* [the Receptive]) come together" (Wei Po-yang, *Ts'an t'ung Ch'i*, quoted in Jung, *Mysterium*, 458, note 11).

NOTES

1. I do not mean to say that maleness and femaleness, even in their biological,

genetic, and physiological aspects, are matters clearly and easily defined for everybody. Put differently, the objective elements taken into account in the subjective definition of one's gender identity are very complex, and many of them remain undiscovered and/or poorly understood. The cases of transsexuals and the old institution of the berdache may be cited as examples of the kinds of complexities involved (LeVay 131-135; Blum). See Walter L. Williams, *The Spirit and the Flesh* (Boston: Beacon Press, 1986); and Ramón Gutiérrez, *When Jesus Came, the Corn Mothers Went Away* (Stanford, CA: Stanford University Press, 1991), pp. 33-35 and 72. Still, short of abandoning all subjectivity in human becoming, the factor of choice must be reckoned within any discussion of gender identity.

2. In using the word "created" here I am aware that I have consistently identified this term as male. Also, I am aware that the forging of one's gendered self is achieved in an active as well as a receptive fashion; this is what *wu-wei* means, an agency that achieves its ends by nonaction — specifically, by receptivity. Paraphrasing John Milton, one could state, "they also act who only stand and wait." I have used creativity as a way to emphasize the need to act consequent upon choice. Obviously, I strongly believe that this action can be either creative or receptive, and that perhaps the receptive will get us where we want to go faster and with less interference.

Bibliography

Abbott, Walter M., S.J., ed. *The Documents of Vatican II.* New York: The America Press, 1966.

Absher, Tom. "Gilgamesh and the Feminine." *Anima*, 15:1 (Fall Equinox, 1988): 20-29.

Apollodorus of Athens. *Gods and Heroes of the Greeks: The Library of Apollodorus*, Michael Simpson, trans. Amherst: University of Massachusetts at Amherst, 1976.

Aquinas, Saint Thomas. *Opera Omnia*, E. Fretté and P. Maré, eds. Paris, 1872-1880.

Arendt, Hannah. *The Life of the Mind: Part 1, Thinking.* New York: Harcourt Brace Jovanovich, 1977.

Aristophanes. *The Plays of Aristophanes*, translated by Benjamin Bickley Rogers. Chicago: Encyclopaedia Britannica, 1952.

Aristotle. *The Complete Works of Aristotle*, Jonathan Barnes, ed. 2 vols. Princeton, N.J.: Princeton University Press, 1984.

Ashtasâhasrikâ prajñâpâramitâ, R. Mitra, ed. Calcutta, 1888.

Augustine, Saint. *Opera Omnia,* in J. P. Migne, ed. *Patrologiae Cursus Completus, Series Latina.* Paris: Garnier, 1844-1855.

Bachelard, Gaston. *The Poetics of Reverie.* Boston: Beacon Press, 1971.

Bailey, Derrick Sherwin. *Sexual Relations in Christian Thought.* New York: Harper & Brothers, 1959.

Barber, Elizabeth Wayland. *Women's Work: The First 20,000 Years.* New York: W.W. Norton & Co., 1994.

Beh, Siew Hwa. "Growing Up with Legends of the Chinese Swordswomen," in Charlene Spretnak, ed., *The Politics of Women's Spirituality.* New York: Anchor Books, 1982.

Belenky, Mary Field, *et al. Women's Ways of Knowing.* New York: Basic Books, 1986.

Berger, John. *Ways of Seeing.* New York: Penguin Books, 1972.

Berkeley, George. *The Principles of Human Knowledge.* Chicago: Encyclopaedia Britannica, 1952.

Bettelheim, Bruno. *The Uses of Enchantment.* New York: Knopf, 1976.

Bharati, Agehananda. *The Tantric Tradition.* New York: Doubleday Anchor, 1970.

Birdwhistell, Ray L. *Kinesics in Context.* New York: Ballantine Books, 1972.

Blum, Deborah. "The Gender Blur." *Utne Reader* (September-October 1968): 45-48.

Blum, Deborah. *Sex on the Brain: The Biological Differences Between Men and Women.* New York: Penguin, 1997.

Boëthius, Anicius M. S. *Boëthius: The Theological Tractates and The Consolation of*

Philosophy, H. F. Stewart and E. K. Paul, eds. "The Loeb Classical Library." Cambridge, MA: Harvard University Press, 1918.

Boswell, John. *Same-Sex Unions in Premodern Europe*. New York: Villard Books, 1994.

Braudel, Fernand. *The Structures of Everyday Life*. 3 vols. New York: Harper & Row, 1981.

Brill, A.A. *The Basic Writings of Sigmund Freud*. New York: The Modern Library, 1938.

Brown, Norman O. *Love's Body*. New York: Random House, 1966.

Brown, Peter. *The Body and Society*. New York: Columbia University Press, 1988.

Brownmiller, Susan. *Against Our Will*. New York: Simon & Schuster, 1975.

Bullough, Vern L., and James Brundage. *Sexual Practices and the Medieval Church*. Buffalo: Prometheus Books, 1982.

Bynum, Caroline Walker. *Holy Feast and Holy Fast: The Religious Significance of Food to Medieval Women*. Berkeley: University of California Press, 1987.

Bynum, Caroline Walker, *et al.*, eds. *Gender and Religion*. Boston: Beacon Press, 1986.

Campbell, Joseph. *Hero with a Thousand Faces*. Princeton, N.J.: Princeton University Press, 1972.

Campbell, Joseph. *Historical Atlas of World Mythology*. New York: Harper & Row, 1988.

Campbell, Joseph. *The Masks of God*, 4 vols. New York: Penguin Books, 1978.

Camus, Albert. *The Rebel*. New York: Vintage, 1956.

Chauvet, Jean-Marie, *et al. Dawn of Art: The Chauvet Cave*. New York: Harry N. Abrams, Inc., 1996.

Chesler, Phyllis. "The Amazon Legacy," in Charlene Spretnak, ed., *The Politics of Women's Spirituality*. New York: Anchor Books, 1982.

Chodorow, Nancy. *The Reproduction of Mothering: Psychoanalysis and the Sociology of Gender*. Berkeley: University of California Press, 1978.

Cicero, Marcus Tullius. *Oeuvres Complètes*. Paris: Firmin-Didot, 1881.

Codex Iuris Canonici [1917]. Madrid: Biblioteca de Autores Cristianos, 1957.

Connell, R.W. "Teaching the Boys: New Research on Masculinity and Gender Strategies for Schools." *Teachers College Record* 98:2 (Winter 1996): 206-235.

Cramer, Phebe, and Katherine A. Hogan, "Sex Differences in Verbal and Play Fantasy." *Developmental Psychology* 1:3 (1975): 145-154.

Crouzel, Henri. *Théologie de l'Image de Dieu chez Origène*. Aubier: Éditions Montaige, 1955.

Daly, Mary. *Gyn/Ecology*. Boston: Beacon Press, 1978.

Davidson, H. R. Ellis. *Scandinavian Mythology*. London: Hamlyn, 1975.

de Beauvoir, Simone. *The Second Sex*. New York: Bantam, 1970.

de Lubac, Henri. *The Eternal Feminine*. New York: Harper & Row, 1971.

D'Emilio, John, and Estelle B. Freedman. *Intimate Matters: A History of Sexuality in America*. New York: Harper & Row, 1988.

Dijkstra, Bram. *Idols of Perversity*. New York: Oxford University Press, 1986.

Dinnerstein, Dorothy. *The Mermaid and the Minotaur*. New York: Harper Colophon, 1977.

Dinter, Paul E. "Christ's Body as Male and Female." *Cross Currents* 44:3 (Fall 1994): 390-399.

Duneier, M. *Slim's Table: Race, Responsibility, and Masculinity*. Chicago: University of Chicago Press, 1992.

Dunnsmith-Burger, Sally M. *A Feminist Metamorphosing of Tree/Cross Symbolism*. Unpublished Masters Thesis. New College of Hofstra University, 1987.

Dworkin, Andrea. *Intercourse*. New York: The Free Press, 1987.

Dworkin, Andrea. *Woman Hating*. New York: E. P. Dutton & Co., 1974.

Efrem, Saint. *Sancti Ephraem Syri Hymni et Sermones*, ed. T. J. Lamy, 4 vols. Mechliniae, Belgium, 1902.

Ehrenreich, Barbara. "The Heart of the Matter." *Ms*. 16:1 (May 1988): 20-21.

Ehrenzweig, Anton. *The Hidden Order of Art*. Berkeley: University of California Press, 1967.

Eiseley, Loren. *The Immense Journey*. New York: Vintage, 1957.

Eliade, Mircea. *Rites and Symbols of Initiation*. New York: Harper Torchbooks, 1965.

Ellis, Lee, and Linda Eberts, eds. *Sexual Orientation: Toward Biological Understanding*. Westport, CT: Praeger Publishers, 1997.

Ellul, Jacques. *The Technological Society*. New York: Random House, 1974.

Engels, Frederick. "The Origin of the Family, Private Property, and the State," in Karl Marx and Frederick Engels, *Selected Works*. New York: International Publishers, 1972.

Engels, Frederick. "The part played by labour in the transition from ape to man" [1876], in Karl Marx and Frederick Engels, *Selected Works*. New York: International Publishers, 1972.

Epstein, Barbara. "Why Post-Structuralism Is a Dead End for Progressive Thought." *Socialist Review* 25:2 (1995): 83-119.

Erikson, Erik H. *Childhood and Society*. New York: Norton, 1963.

Erikson, Erik H. *Identity: Youth and Crisis*. New York: Norton, 1968.

Euripides. *The Plays of Euripides*, translated by Edward P. Coleridge. Chicago: Encyclopaedia Britannica, 1952.

Eusebius of Caesarea. *The History of the Church from Christ to Constantine*. New York: Barnes & Noble, 1995.

"An exchange: Mothering and the Reproduction of Power." *Socialist Review* 14:6 (November-December 1984): 121-130.

Faricy, Robert, S.J. "The Person-Nature Split: Ecology, Women, and Human Life." *The Teilhard Review* 23:2 (Summer 1988): 33-44.

Fausto-Sterling, Anne. *Myths of Gender*. New York: Basic Books, 1985.

Frantz, Marie-Louise von. "The Process of Individuation," in C. G. Jung *et al*. *Man and His Symbols*. Garden City, N.Y.: Doubleday & Co., 1964.

Freud, Sigmund. *Delusion and Dreams*. Boston: Beacon Press, 1956.

Freud, Sigmund. "Medusa's Head," vol. 18 of *Collected Works*, Standard Edition, James Strachey, ed. London: Hogarth Press, 1961.

Freud, Sigmund. "Some Psychical Consequences of the Anatomical Distinction between the Sexes" [1925], vol. 19 of *Collected Works*, Standard Edition, James Strachey, ed. London: Hogarth Press, 1961.

Freud, Sigmund. "The 'Uncanny,'" vol. 17 of *Collected Works*, Standard Edition, James Strachey, ed. London: Hogarth Press, 1961.

Galen. *Opera Omnia*, 20 vols., C.G. Kuhn, ed. Leipzig, 1821-1833.

Garai, Josef E., and Amram Scheinfeld. "Sex Differences in Mental and Behavioral Traits." *Genetic Psychology Monographs* 77:2 (1968): 169-299.

Gibbon, Edward. *The Decline and Fall of the Roman Empire*, 2 vols. Chicago: Encyclopaedia Britannica, 1952.

Gilligan, Carol. *In a Different Voice.* Cambridge, MA: Harvard University Press, 1982.

Gimbutas, Marija. *The Goddesses and Gods of Old Europe.* Berkeley: University of California Press, 1982.

Gimbutas, Marija. "Women and Culture in Goddess-Oriented Old Europe," in *The Politics of Women's Spirituality*, Charlene Spretnak, ed. New York: Anchor Books, 1982.

Goethe, Johann Wolfgang von. *Faust.* New York: Alfred A. Knopf, 1941.

Gold, Penny S. "The Marriage of Mary and Joseph in the Twelfth-Century Ideology of Marriage," in Vern L. Bullough and James Brundage, *Sexual Practices and the Medieval Church.* Buffalo: Prometheus Books, 1982.

Gordimer, Nadine. "Home," in *Fiction 100*, James H. Pickering, ed. 6th ed. New York: Macmillan Publishing Co., 1992, p. 534-543.

Gordon, Haim. "Learning to Think: Arendt on Education for Democracy." *Educational Forum* 53:1 (Fall 1988): 49-62.

Gottlieb, Roger. "Mothering and the Reproduction of Power." *Socialist Review* 14:5 (September-October 1984): 93-119.

Götz, Ignacio L. *Creativity: Theoretical and Socio-Cosmic Reflections.* Washington, D.C.: University Press of America, 1978.

Götz, Ignacio L. "Education and Masculine/Feminine Consciousness." *Educational Theory* 36:1 (Winter 1986): 23-32.

Götz, Ignacio L. "On Children and Television." *The Elementary School Journal* 75:7 (April 1975): 415-418.

Götz, Ignacio L. "On Defining Creativity." *Journal of Aesthetics and Art Criticism* 39:3 (Spring 1981): 297-301.

Grant, Michael. *Myths of the Greeks and Romans.* New York: New American Library, 1962.

Graves, Robert. *The Greek Myths*, 2 vols. New York: George Braziller, Inc., 1955.

Grimm's Fairy Tales. New York: Random House, 1972.

Groth, A. Nicholas. *Men Who Rape.* New York: Plenum Press, 1979.

Grumet, Madeleine R. *Bitter Milk.* Amherst: The University of Massachusetts Press, 1988.

Gutiérrez, Ramón. *When Jesus Came, the Corn Mothers Went Away.* Stanford, CA: Stanford University Press, 1991.

Heidegger, Martin. *Existence and Being.* Chicago: Regnery, 1949.

Henderson, Joseph L. "Ancients Myths and Modern Man," in C. G. Jung *et al.*, *Man and His Symbols.* Garden City, N.Y.: Doubleday & Co., 1964.

Hesse, Hermann. *Demian.* New York: Bantam Books, 1970.

Hesse, Hermann. *Narcissus and Goldmund.* New York: Farrar, Straus & Giroux, 1968.

Hirson, Roger O. *Pippin.* Music and lyrics by Stephen Schwartz. New York: Music Theatre International, 1975.

Hölderlin, Friedrich. *Werke.* Berlin: Propyläen-Verlag, 1914.

Homer. *The Iliad*, E. V. Rieu, trans. London: Penguin Books, 1950.

Homer. *The Odyssey of Homer*, Robert Fitzgerald, trans. Garden City, N.Y.: Doubleday, 1963.

Hong Kingston, Maxine. *The Woman Warrior.* New York: Knopff, 1977.

Horney, Karen. "The Flight from Womanhood," in Jeane Baker Miller, ed., *Psychoanalysis and Women.* Baltimore: Penguin Books, 1973.

Husserl, Edmund. *Cartesian Meditations.* The Hague: Martinus Nijhoff, 1960.

Husserl, Edmund. *Ideas*. London: Collier-Macmillan, 1962.

Huston, Nancy. "The Matrix of War: Mothers and Heroes," in Susan Rubin Suleiman, ed., *The Female Body in Western Culture*. Cambridge, MA: Harvard University Press, 1986.

Huston, Nancy. "Tales of War and Tears of Women," in Judith Stiehm, ed., *Women and Men's Wars*. New York: Pergamon Press, 1983.

Illich, Ivan. *Vernacular Gender*. University Park: Pennsylvania State University, 1982.

Ionesco, Eugène. *Rhinocéros*, 2nd ed., R.Y. Ellison, S.C. Goding, and A. Raffanel, eds. New York: Holt, Rinehart & Winston, 1976.

Irenæus of Lyons, *Adversus Hæreses*. English translation in A. Roberts and W.H. Rambaut, eds. *The Ante-Nicene Library: The Writings of Irenaeus*. Edinburgh: T. & T. Clark, 1869.

Isidore of Seville, *Opera*, in J. P. Migne, ed. *Patrologiae Cursus Completus*, Series Latina. Paris: Garnier, 1844-1855.

Jantz, Harold. *The Mothers in FAUST*. Baltimore: The Johns Hopkins University Press, 1969.

Johnson, Mark. *The Body in the Mind*. Chicago: The University of Chicago Press, 1987.

Jonas, Hans. *The Gnostic Religion*. Boston: Beacon Press, 1963.

Jung, Carl G. *The Collected Works of C.G. Jung*. Princeton, N.J.: Princeton University Press, 1959.

Jung, Carl G. *Mysterium Coniunctionis*, 2nd ed. Princeton, N.J.: Princeton University Press, 1970.

Jung, Carl G. *Septem Sermones ad Mortuos*, in *Memories, Dreams, Reflections*. *Collected Works*, vol. 5. New York: Bollingen Series XX, 1956.

Jung, Carl G., et al. *Man and His Symbols*. Garden City, N.Y.: Doubleday & Co., 1964.

Juvenal, Decimus. *Satires*, G. G. Ramsay, trans. "Loeb Classical Library." Cambridge, MA: Harvard University Press, 1918.

Karapâtrî, Swâmî. "Krishna tattva." *Siddhantâ* 5 (1944-1945).

Karapâtrî, Swâmî. "Lingopâsanâ-rahasya." *Siddhantâ* 2 (1941-1942).

Kierkegaard, Sóren. "Diary of a Seducer," in *Either/Or*, 2 vols. New York: Doubleday Anchor, 1959.

Kimmel, Michael S. "Women-hating in Perspective." *Psychology Today* XXI, No.4 (April 1987).

The Koran, with Parallel Arabic Text, N. J. Dawood, trans. London: Penguin Books, 1995.

Laqueur, Thomas. *Making Sex*. Cambridge, MA: Harvard University Press, 1990.

Leach, Edmund R. "Magical Hair," in *Myth and Cosmos*, John Middleton, ed. Austin, TX: University of Texas Press, 1967.

Leo the Great. *Epistulae et Sermones*, in J. P. Migne, ed. *Patrologiae Cursus Completus*, Series Latina. Paris: Garnier, 1844-1855.

Lerner, Gerda. *The Creation of Patriarchy*. New York: Oxford University Press, 1986.

LeVay, Simon. *The Sexual Brain*. Cambridge, MA: MIT Press, 1993.

Lévi-Strauss, Claude. *The Savage Mind*. Chicago: Chicago University Press, 1968.

Liber Usualis, edited by the Benedictines of Solesmes. Tournai, Belgium: Desclée & Co., 1961.

Lichtheim, Miriam. *Ancient Egyptian Literature*, 2 vols. Berkeley: University of California Press, 1973.

114   Bibliography

Lincoln, Bruce. *Emerging from the Chrysalis: Studies in Rituals of Women's Initiation.* Cambridge, MA: Harvard University Press, 1981.

Lombard, Peter. *Sententiarum Libri Quatuor.* 2 vols. Quaracchi, 1916.

Loomis, Roger Sherman, and Laura Hibbard, eds. *Medieval Romances.* New York: The Modern Library, 1957.

MacPherson, Vicki Rourke. "Newgrange: The Illuminated Spiral." *Anima* 11:2 (1985): 117-124.

Macy, Joanna. "Perfection of Wisdom: Mother of All Buddhas." *Anima* 3:1 (1976): 75-80.

Magolda, Marcia B. Baxter. *Knowing and Reasoning in College: Gender-related Patterns in Students' Intellectual Development.* San Francisco: Jossey-Bass, 1992.

Maimonides, Moses. *Epistles of Maimonides,* translated by Abraham Halkin. Philadelphia: The Jewish Publication Society of America, 1985.

Maimonides, Moses. "The Thirteen Principles," in *Judaism,* Arthur Hertzberg, ed. New York: Braziller, 1962.

Mairs, Nancy. "I Have Not Yet Begun to Speak." *Anima* 14:2 (Spring 1988): 75-86.

Marx, Karl and Engels, Frederick. *The German Ideology,* in *Karl Marx and Frederick Engels, Collected Works,* vol. 5. New York: International Publishers, 1976.

May, Rollo. *Love and Will.* New York: W.W. Norton Co., 1969.

McLuhan, Marshall. *Understanding Media.* New York: McGraw-Hill, 1964.

Mead, Margaret. *Male and Female.* New York: William Morrow & Co., 1949.

Menon, Shanti. "Hominid Hardware." *Discover* 18 (May 1997).

Merleau-Ponty, Maurice. *Phenomenology of Perception.* London: Routledge & Kegan Paul, 1962.

Miller, Jeane Baker. *Toward a New Psychology of Women.* Boston: Beacon Press, 1976.

Mitamura, Taisuke. *Chinese Eunuchs.* Rutland, VT: Charles E. Tuttle Co., Inc., 1970.

Moreau, Jacques-Louis, *Histoire naturelle de la femme* (Paris, 1803).

Morgan, Robin, "The Demon Lover." *Ms.* 12:9 (March 1989): 68-72.

Müller, F. Max. *The Upanishads,* 2 vols. New York: Dover Publications, 1962.

Mumford, Lewis. "Technics and the Nature of Man," in Carl Mitcham and Robert Mackey, eds., *Philosophy and Technology.* New York: The Free Press, 1983.

Nadeau, Robert L. *S/he Brain: Science, Sexual Politics, and the Myths of Feminism.* Westport, CT: Praeger Publishers, 1996.

Nâgârjuna, *Lokâtîtastava* and *Sûnytâsaptati,* in *Master of Wisdom. Writings of the Buddhist Master Nâgârjuna.* Oakland, CA: Dharma Publishing, 1986.

Nehamas, Alexander. *Nietzsche: Life as Literature.* Cambridge, MA: Harvard University Press, 1985.

Neumann, Erich. *Art and the Creative Unconscious.* Princeton, N.J.: Princeton University Press, 1959.

Neumann, Erich. *The Fear of the Feminine.* Princeton, N.J.: Princeton University Press, 1994.

Neumann, Erich. *The Origins and History of Consciousness.* Princeton, N.J.: Princeton University Press, 1954.

Nichols, Sister Marilyn, SSJ. "Toward an Understanding of the Feminine in Teilhard." *Anima* 7:2 (1981): 114-120.

Nietzsche, Friedrich. *Beyond Good and Evil.* Chicago: Regnery, 1966.

Nietzsche, Friedrich. *The Gay Science.* New York: Vintage, 1974.

Nietzsche, Friedrich. *On the Genealogy of Morals* and *Ecce Homo.* New York:

Vintage, 1967.

Nietzsche, Friedrich. *Thus Spoke Zarathustra*, Walter Kaufmann, trans. and ed. New York: Vintage, 1966.

Nietzsche, Friedrich. *The Will to Power*, Walter Kaufmann, ed. New York: Vintage, 1968.

Noble, David F. *The Religion of Technology*. New York: Alfred A. Knopf, 1997.

Noble, David F. *A World Without Women*. New York: Alfred A. Knopf, 1992.

Oates, Joyce Carol. "Success and the Pseudonymous Writer: Turning Over a New Self," *The New York Times Book Review*, December 6, 1987, p. 14.

Ortega y Gasset, José. *Man and People*. New York: W. W. Norton & Co., 1963.

Ortega y Gasset, José. "Meditación de la técnica," in *Ensimismamiento y Alteración* [1939], vol. 5 of *Obras Completas*. Madrid: Revista de Occidente, 1970.

Ortner, Sherry B. "Is Female to Male as Nature Is to Culture?" in *Woman, Culture and Society*, M. Z. Rosaldo and L. Lamphere, eds. Stanford: Stanford University Press, 1974.

Ovid. *Metamorphoses*, Rolfe Humphries, trans. Bloomington, IN: Indiana University Press, 1964.

Pagels, Elaine. *The Gnostic Gospels*. New York: Random House, 1979.

Paglia, Camille. *Sexual Personae*. New York: Vintage, 1990.

Perrault's Fairy Tales. New York: Dover Publications, 1969.

Perry, William G. *Forms of Intellectual and Ethical Development in the College Years*. New York: Holt, Rinehart & Winston, 1970.

Pfeiffer, John E. *The Creative Explosion*. New York: Harper & Row, 1982.

Phillips, John A. *Eve: A History of an Idea*. New York: Harper & Row, 1984.

Piaget, Jeane. *The Origins of Intelligence in Children*. New York: W. W. Norton, 1963.

Plato. *The Dialogues of Plato*, B. Jowett trans. Oxford: Oxford University Press, 1871.

Plutarch. *The Lives of the Noble Grecians and Romans*. New York: Modern Library, 1992.

Proclus. *Epicorum Graecorum Fragmenta*, G. Kinkel, ed.

Quintus Smyrnaeus. *Posthomerica* (The Fall of Troy), Arthur S. Way, trans. Cambridge, MA: Harvard University Press, 1955.

Ranke-Heinemann, Uta. *Eunuchs for the Kingdom of Heaven*. New York: Doubleday, 1990.

Reed, Bika. *Rebel in the Soul*. New York: Inner Traditions International, Ltd., 1978.

Robinson, James M., ed. *The Nag Hammadi Library*. New York: Harper & Row, 1978.

Rose, Susan. "Child Sacrifice: Projective Christianity." *Anima* 20:1 (Fall 1993): 5-18.

Roussel, Pierre. *Du système physique et morale de la femme* (1775).

Rubin, Gayle. "The Traffic in Women," in Rayna Reiter, ed., *Toward an Anthropology of Women*. New York: Monthly Review, 1975.

Rubinstein, Mark. "The Fascinating King Named Kong." *Psychology Today* 10:8 (January 1977): 44-48, 111.

Ruether, Rosemary Radford. *Sexism and God-Talk*. Boston: Beacon Press, 1983.

Rufus, Musonius. *Fragments*, in "Musonius Rufus. The Roman Socrates," Cora B. Lutz, ed. *Yale Classical Studies* 10 (1947).

Sandars, N. K. *The Epic of Gilgamesh*. Baltimore: Penguin, 1972.

Sanday, Peggy R. "Rape and the Silencing of the Feminine," in Sylvana Tomaselli and Roy Porter, eds., *Rape*. London: Basil Blackwell Ltd, 1986.

Sartre, Jean-Paul. *Being and Nothingness*. New York: Washington Square Press, 1966.

116 Bibliography

Sartre, Jean-Paul. *The Imagination*. Ann Arbor: The University of Michigan Press, 1972.

Schafer, Edward H. *The Divine Woman*. Berkeley: University of California Press, 1973.

Scheler, Max. *Ressentiment*. New York: Schocken Books, 1972.

Sebold, Alice. "Speaking of the Unspeakable." *The New York Times Magazine*, February 26, 1989.

Shakespeare, William. *The Plays and Sonnets of William Shakespeare*, William George Clarke and William Aldis Wright, eds., 2 vols. Chicago: Encyclopaedia Britannica, 1952.

Sheets-Johnstone, Maxine. "Corporeal Archetypes and Power: Preliminary Clarifications and Considerations of Sex." *Hypatia* 7:3 (Summer 1992): 39-76.

Silverstein, Shel. *The Giving Tree*. New York: Harper & Row, 1964.

Singer, June. *Androgyny*. New York: Doubleday, 1976.

Slater, Philip. *The Pursuit of Loneliness*. Boston: Beacon Press, 1970.

Sophocles. *The Three Theban Plays*, Robert Fagles, trans. New York: Penguin Books, 1982.

Spretnak, Charlene, ed. *The Politics of Women's Spirituality*. New York: Anchor Books, 1982.

Stackhouse, Max L. *The Ethics of Necropolis*. Boston: Beacon Press, 1971.

Stannard, Una. *Mrs Man*. San Francisco: Germainbooks, 1977.

Stein, Arlene. "Sisters and Queers." *Socialist Review* 22:1 (January-March 1992): 33-55.

Suetonius, Gaius. *The Twelve Caesars*. London: Penguin Books, 1957.

Tao Te Ching, in *A Buddhist Bible*, Dwight Goddard, ed. Boston: Beacon Press, 1966.

Teilhard de Chardin, Pierre. "The Eternal Feminine," in *Writings in Time of War*. London: Collins, 1968.

Teilhard de Chardin, Pierre. "The Spirit of the Earth," in *Human Energy*. New York: Harcourt Brace Jovanovich, Inc., 1969.

Tertullian, Quintus Septimius Florens. *Opera Omnia. Corpus Christianorum*, Series Latina. 2 vols. Turnhout: Brepols, 1954.

Thomas, D. Winton. *Documents from Old Testament Times*. New York: Harper Torchbooks, 1958.

Tomaselli, Sylvana and Roy, Porter, eds. *Rape*. London: Basil Blackwell Ltd., 1986.

Trebicot, Joyce. "Sex Roles: The Argument from Nature," in Mary Briody Mahowald, ed., *Philosophy of Woman*. Indianapolis: Hackett, 1978.

Turley, Donna. "The Feminist Debate on Pornography: An Unorthodox Interpretation." *Socialist Review* 16:3-4 (May-August 1986).

Twain, Mark. *The Family Mark Twain*, 2 vols. New York: Harper & Row, 1972.

Tyack, David B. *The One Best System*. Cambridge, MA: Harvard University Press, 1974.

Unamuno, Miguel de. *Amor y Pedagogía*. Madrid: Editorial Magisterio Español, 1967.

Unamuno, Miguel de. *Tragic Sense of Life*. New York: Dover Publications, 1954.

Vaidyarâj, Pandit Vanshîdhar Sukul. *Vâmamârga*. Allahabad: Kalyân Mandir, 1951.

Valéry, Paul. *The Collected Works of Paul Valéry*, 15 vols., Jackson Mathews, ed. New York: Bollingen, 1964.

Van Kaam, Adrian. "Sex and Existence," in Nathaniel Lawrence and Daniel O'Connor, eds., *Readings in Existential Phenomenology*. Englewood Cliffs, N.J.: Prentice-Hall, 1967.

Vâtsyâyana. *Kâma Sûtra*. New York: Castle Books, 1963.

Venette, Nicolas. *Conjugal Love; or The Pleasures of the Marriage Bed Considered in Several Lectures on Human Generation*. London, 1750.

Wadsworth, Wallace. *Paul Bunyan: Hero of the Lumber Woods*. New York: Doubleday, 1960.

Washburn, S. L. and Ruth Moore. *Ape into Human,* 2nd ed. Boston: Little, Brown & Co., 1980.

Wehr, Demaris. "Uses and Abuses of Jung's Psychology for Women: Animus." *Anima* 12:1 (Fall Equinox 1985).

Weideger, Paula. "Womb Worship." *Ms*. 16:8 (February 1988): 54-57.

Weininger, Otto. *Sex and Character*. New York: A. L. Burt Company, n.d. (*ca.* 1906).

Wenke, Robert J. *Patterns in History,* 4th ed. New York: Oxford University Press, 1998.

Wheelis, Allen. *The Moralist*. Baltimore: Penguin Books, 1973.

Whitmont, Edward C. *Return to the Goddess*. New York: Crossroad, 1982.

Williams, Walter L. *The Spirit and the Flesh*. Boston: Beacon Press, 1986.

Wolkstein, Diane, and Samuel Noah Kramer. *Inanna: Queen of Heaven and Earth*. New York: HarperCollins, 1983.

Woodman, Marion. *The Pregnant Virgin*. Toronto: Inner City Books, 1985.

Yebenes, Pablo Solo de Zaldivar. *La Cueva de Nerja*. Granada: Foundation of the Cave of Nerja, 1977.

Zilboorg, Gregory. "Masculine and Feminine." *Psychiatry* 7:3 (August 1944): 257-296.

Zola, Émile. *Nana*, George Holden, trans. New York: Penguin, 1972.

Index

About the Author

IGNACIO L. GÖTZ is Professor of Philosophy and Teaching Fellow at New College, Hofstra University, where he serves as Coordinator of the Programs in Humanities and Creative Studies. Among his earlier books are *The Psychedelic Teacher, Creativity: Theoretical and Socio-Cosmic Reflections*, and *Conceptions of Happiness*.

ISBN 0-275-96566-X

HARDCOVER BAR CODE